Brief Strategic C

Brief Strategic Coaching

The problem resolution process that inspired brief and solution-focused thinking

by
Andrew Armatas

 Open University Press

Open University Press
McGraw Hill
8th Floor, 338 Euston Road
London
England
NW1 3BH

email: enquiries@openup.co.uk
world wide web: www.openup.co.uk

First edition published 2021

A catalogue record of this book is available from the British Library

ISBN-13: 9780335249435
ISBN-10: 0335249434
eISBN: 9780335249442

Library of Congress Cataloging-in-Publication Data
CIP data applied for

Typeset by Transforma Pvt. Ltd., Chennai, India

Praise Page

Steeped in academic rigour and practitioner experience, this book makes a compelling case for a brief strategic coaching approach, with plenty of client examples and tips for putting it into practice. I wish I'd had my hands on this before - my leader clients certainly would have benefited! A highly valuable addition to the coach's toolkit.

Liz Hall, Editor of Coaching at Work magazine,
Author of Mindful Coaching and Coach Your Team

Andrew Armatas' brief strategic coping book is must have reading for any coach. He explains very well with easy-to-understand case examples. This book also discusses what causes the solution to become a new problem for clients. Develop your knowledge of coaching by better understanding the brief strategic approach.

Sandi Kartasasmita, M.Psi., Psychologist., Psychotherapist,
Lecturer at Universitas Tarumanagara, Board Member of
Indonesian Coach Practitioners Association (APCI)

This book tells us why "solutions create problems"; this insightful book gives you bundles of practical strategies to tackle this conundrum head-on. Coaching practices that reframe what you already know, and some which feel counter-intuitive but highlight effective. Worth adding to your coaching toolkit.

Professor Tony Wall, International Centre for
Thriving at the University of Chester

Andrew Armatas has produced a thought-provoking and perfectly accessible book explaining why we fail to solve problems when we focus entirely on their solutions and outlining strategies to successfully achieve desired change. Engaging and practical, this book is an invaluable guide for coaches and practitioners who work with clients wishing to break free from ineffective problem-solving strategies.

Dr Christiana Iordanou, Lecturer in Psychology, University
of Kent; Co-author of Values and Ethics in Coaching

Andrew Armatas offers a much needed, novel perspective on coaching, casting the focus on the attempted solutions of a problem, rather than the problem itself. Written in an accessible and engaging manner, packed with practical examples and insightful suggestions, Brief Strategic Coaching champions reflexive interactions with the problem and everyone involved with it, in order to help the coachee escape a vicious circle of attempted solutions that perpetuate a problem. Concise in size yet rich in detail, it is a must-read text for novice and experienced coaches, supervisors, and trainers who wish to enhance their knowledge with fresh and insightful coaching strategies.

Dr Ioanna Iordanou, Reader in Human Resource Management (Coaching and Mentoring), International Centre for Coaching and Mentoring Studies, Oxford Brookes Business School and co-author of Values and Ethics in Coaching (Sage, 2017)

As a coaching psychologist, I have found this book a useful companion to my coaching literature collection. The solution we introduce to solve a problem often creates more problems. It is a good anecdote to any solution focused coaches. The brief strategic approach would certainly be a necessary tool to add to their coaching toolbox as well as mine in dealing with clients who get stuck.

Professor Ho Chung Law, Empsy® Cambridge Coaching Psychology Group, www.empsy.com

In his book "Brief Strategic Coaching", Andrew Armatas starts with a summary of the important work of the Mental Research Institute Palo Alto MRI (Watzlawick, Haley, Bateson, etc) and Steve de Shazer and describes a clear model of strategic coaching with many brief illustrative transcripts of coaching interactions. I highly recommend this book to everyone who is interested in learning to apply the strategic approaches of Milton Erickson in coaching.

Bernhard Trenkle, President ISH International Society of Hypnosis Member BOD of Milton Erickson Foundation, Phoenix

To Marcella, the one and only …

Contents

1 The Brief Strategic Approach: An Overview

In the first half of the previous century, psychoanalysis was king. It was the dominant mode of psychiatry and remained so for many years. However, in the 1950s, the first seeds of dissatisfaction with the prevailing analytical exploration and its slow process had started to sprout (Nardone 2004, Kaslow 2007). Harry Stack Sullivan, an American psychiatrist, was one of the first to plant those early seeds by stressing the importance of interpersonal interaction in psychopathology, a concept that had been overlooked in favour of inner individual analysis (Morgan 2014). His different approach with clients can be detected in his preference for the term 'problems of living' in place of other terms that denote illness.

Sullivan deviated from classic psychoanalytical thinking and offered a systemic view of human experience (Kanter 2013). To him, disease was not an individual matter but an interpersonal one, and what happened between people mattered more than what happened within them. He suggested focusing on the interaction between the internal and external world rather than directing attention to early childhood experiences, fantasy life and the inner world (Evans 1996). Sullivan's teachings impacted contemporary psychology and influenced future generations. One of those influenced by Sullivan's ideas was Gregory Bateson.

The Bateson Project

In 1954, Bateson, a well-respected British anthropologist, received a grant to investigate communication patterns in families who had a member being treated for schizophrenia (Bateson et al. 1963, Leeds-Hurwitz 2005, Leeds-Hurwitz 2016). Just like Sullivan, Bateson's view was that psychological wellbeing could not be considered as simply a matter of individual mental processes. He saw the world as a network of systems interacting with one another. Bateson posited that, since communication and behaviour affect one another, much of psychopathology has its roots in that interaction (Tramonti 2018).

Bateson was not alone in his endeavours. John Weakland, Jay Haley, William Fry and Don Jackson, who formed his research group (Ray 2018), focused their decade-long inquiry on communication patterns and context. Prolific writers as they were, their investigation became one of the most influential research projects conducted in the behavioural realm. Together, they developed a theory of schizophrenia that had its roots in the way family members communicated with the 'patient-member' (Bateson et al. 1963). They concluded that conflicting and emotionally distressing messages – known as double binds – contributed to the aetiology of schizophrenia (Bateson et al. 1956, Watzlawick 1963, Watzlawick et al. 1974/2011, Weakland 1979, Rieber and Vetter 1995, Gibney 2006, Watzlawick et al. 1967/2011).

Although the double-bind theory of schizophrenia did not catch on, it directed attention to the importance of identifying and modifying problematic family interactions. Their landmark article 'Toward a Theory of Schizophrenia' (Bateson et al. 1956), despite its narrow focus, had a wider impact on mental health. It laid the foundation for a new understanding of human behaviour that incorporated a systems perspective and it also suggested a base for marriage and family therapy, as well as brief therapies, to develop. It contradicted the normal practice of therapeutically working solely with the individual with the problem. Bateson saw the problem through a relational and social context. Such was his influence that he is credited by many as being the father of family therapy. His research project remains one of the most influential sources of systemic and interactional approaches to human behaviour.

The Mental Research Institute

In 1958, Don Jackson founded the Mental Research Institute (MRI) in Palo Alto, also known as the Palo Alto Group (Weakland and Ray 1995, Nichols and Schwartz 2005, Quick 2008, Ray 2007). It quickly established itself as the place of choice for therapists who aspired to be on the cutting edge of psychology research and practice. Many notable experts attended the Institute, such as Jay Haley, Virginia Satir, John Weakland, Paul Watzlawick, Arthur Bodin, Janet Beavin, Jules Riskin and Carlos Sluzki (Ray 2016). Their focus was not limited to Bateson's work on communication patterns and paradoxes associated with schizophrenia (Weakland et al. 1977). The role of biology and intrapsychic factors was downplayed and Sullivan's interpersonal principles were placed in the forefront (Sullivan 1953). The MRI staff shifted to a more social view of behaviour, where both the creation of problems and their solutions resulted from interactions between individuals (Weakland et al. 1974, Nardone 2004).

It comes to no surprise that Don Jackson dedicated himself to the interpersonal and interactional aspects of behaviour, since he was trained and supervised by Harry Stack Sullivan. However, one significant aspect differentiated the way these two experts worked. Sullivan saw individuals in isolation, away from their families, and he used data from the past to infer problem-maintaining interpersonal factors. Jackson, on the other hand, focused on the actual relationship between the client and other individuals in the here and now (Ray 2004).

There is an interesting story about how Don Jackson conducted one of the first conjoint therapy sessions. A young female with psychosis was making

Preface

Just prior to embarking on this book, I had completed a chapter about a performance solution that backfired at Microsoft (Armatas 2021). In the face of increasing competition, one of Microsoft's solutions was the introduction of a performance review system known as stack ranking. This kind of review system only allows for a predetermined number of people to be rated highly whereas the rest are allocated to lower categories regardless of their performance. This led to a shift in personnel behaviour that negatively impacted company culture and bottom line. Employees started to compete against each other rather than against other businesses; self-interest superseded team work, sabotage replaced collaboration and 'playing it safe' substituted innovation. The filed lawsuits from former employees that were linked to the specific performance review system further confirmed that the attempted solution had become a considerable problem. Microsoft eventually abandoned stack ranking and adopted a mindset that followed an entirely different direction.

At the core of brief strategic work, introduced by the Mental Research Institute (MRI) more than half a century ago, lies the idea that problems are generated by our very attempts to solve them. Since the problem lies in the solution, it is the attempted solution that determines the nature of the intervention. The strategic process of exploring how clients are trying to handle their difficulties and disrupting the faulty solution pattern by introducing a new solution strategy may seem a simple structure, but it has its fair share of difficulties. The new solution is often radically different than what was previously applied, and we need to get our clients, employees or students on board to go against their instincts and act counterintuitively.

The brief strategic approach is a problem resolution process model with its motto being: *if there's no complaint, there's no problem* (Fisch and Schlanger 1999). Since coaching is much more than problem-solving, one may conclude that if there's no problem, there's no need for brief strategic work. Although this may be viewed as a limitation, it can also be considered an advantage since the strategic model can lend itself as an additional tool to a professional's repertoire without excluding current ways of working.

Theory is always better understood when being practised. My intention, from the very beginning, has been to offer a practical take on a classic idea that has inspired many brief, solution-focused and systemic approaches that are widely in use today. I encourage you to give it a go while keeping an open mind as it may challenge the way you think and/or have been trained about the change process. I hope you'll find this book a useful addition to your professional collection and that it will motivate you to use the brief strategic approach with clients or employees who seem to be stuck in a problem-maintenance cycle and, despite their best efforts (or yours), remark how "the more they try, the worse it gets". In the face of problem persistence, an illogical route may just be the most logical way to go.

good progress with Jackson's help. As a result, Jackson asked the young woman's mother to allow her daughter to come to the next session alone. The mother refused to follow Jackson's advice to stay at home. Irritated with the mother's non-compliance, he then invited her to join her daughter's session. It was to become one of the first family sessions to be documented. Jackson was intrigued with the results and began experimenting with family sessions. Such was the influence of MRI in the development of family therapy that it conducted the first family therapy training programme funded by the US and published the first family therapy journal, *Family Process* (Ray 2004).

The MRI Brief Therapy Center

In 1967, the Brief Therapy Center was launched at the Mental Research Institute. The core members were Richard Fisch, John Weakland and Paul Watzlawick. The brief therapy project had one goal: to study ways of doing therapy briefly (Fisch et al. 1982, Fisch and Schlanger 1999, Rohrbaugh and Shoham 2001, Rohrbaugh 2018). One can appreciate the contrast with the prevailing long-term treatments offered by psychoanalysis. Change and brevity were contradictory concepts at the time and to offer therapy designed with brevity in mind was novel. However, there was a man known for his novelty, and brevity was already part of his practice. His name was Milton Erickson.

No one influenced the MRI group more than Milton Erickson, an American psychiatrist, who rose to fame as a result of his innovative psychotherapeutic and hypnotic practices. His impact goes back to the Bateson project, where he acted as a consultant. He had a significant bearing on transforming the process of change and the conduct of therapy (Cade 1987, Cade and O'Hanlon 1993). Erickson's approach was unorthodox to say the least (Haley 1973) and, for his heretic stance, the American Medical Association threatened to revoke his licence. He employed hypnosis when hypnosis was forbidden. He offered direction when only reflection and interpretation were encouraged. He did brief therapy when brief therapy was condemned. He would schedule sessions irregularly when fixed weekly sessions were the norm. Session duration was also malleable. With some of his clients, Erickson would work within the traditional 50-minute sessions but with others sessions would be only a few minutes while, on other occasions, he would conduct sessions that lasted for hours (Haley 1993/2013).

Erickson was flexible and would tailor therapy to his clients' needs. Depending on what he perceived as most beneficial, he would offer directives directly or indirectly, conduct brief or longer-term therapy and utilize whatever the client brought to the session, or even use himself as a means of influence. The latter approach is known as utilization (Erickson 1959/2009, Roffman 2008). Utilization is a foundational concept in the Ericksonian approach. It involves the creative acceptance and use of any behaviour, thought or emotion the client brings to the session, utilizing whatever happens during the session and, when necessary, using the therapist themself in the service of client goal attainment. Erickson also deviated from the reigning belief that the unconscious mind is a dark-natured reservoir of thoughts, feelings and urges. Instead, he viewed it as a positive source with many valuable resources. For years, Haley and Weakland travelled to study alongside Erickson and applied many of his ideas and techniques (Haley 1993, Haley 2013).

Having established Erickson as a key influence, let us return to the Brief Therapy Center in Palo Alto. The Center's staff investigated what could be achieved if therapy were limited to no more than 10 sessions (de Shazer et al. 1986, Rohrbaugh and Shoham 2001, Quick 2008). It is important to clarify that the brief therapy approach at MRI's Brief Therapy Center was not the result of time constraints; nor was it designed from necessity or the outcome of drop-out rates. Brevity was a choice; it was a matter of mindset and a way of solving problems. It was assumed that therapy can be brief and change can be brought about sooner than previously deemed possible. Since problems were viewed as social in cause and origin, and not as the result of intrapsychic conflicts, it was believed that they would respond quickly to focused interventions (Bavelas et al. 1992, Watzlawick and Weakland 1977). In addition to the limited number of sessions, MRI therapists were also flexible with session scheduling. Sessions were not necessarily scheduled on a weekly basis but could be spread over months, depending on what would maximize the likelihood of change.

The goal of MRI therapists was to focus on the presenting complaint (Eubanks 2002). There was a clear departure from the traditional habit of exploring past childhood experiences and deep-seated causes of behaviour (Keeney and Keeney 2012). They moved away from analysing, interpreting and creating insights. They refrained from making assumptions about what is normal or not, they downplayed pathology and they chose to hone in on the observable (Nardone 2004, Nardone and Portelli 2005, Klaij 2016). They believed that the problems clients bring to therapy exist in the here and now, not in the past, and so do their solutions (Weakland et al. 1974, Fisch et al. 1982). The understanding of this approach is that a client with a problem is doing something wrong that is maintaining it or making it worse. The task is to help clients identify what they are doing wrong and help them to change their interactive behaviour by doing something different. The purpose of MRI's brief therapy, therefore, was to resolve the original complaint to the client's satisfaction. If that could be achieved through a simple directive, then that would be their number one choice. They were more focused on techniques that bring change and resolve problems than on theories (Piercy et al. 1996).

Another important premise of the MRI's brief strategic approach is the constructivist perspective that there are many views of reality. According to this approach, one needs to attend to how clients view their problems in addition to what they are doing to solve them. Assigning tasks and reframing with the aim to change perspectives is part of the brief strategic process (Coyne 1985, Flaskas 1992, Quick 2008). Finally, the MRI model differs from the traditional approach by the manner in which communication is viewed (Bavelas et al. 1992, McKergow 2013). In traditional therapy, communication is mostly information transmission. The client describes the current problem and recounts their background history and emotions while the therapist provides a diagnosis, and offers insight and interpretations. The Palo Alto group, however, saw communication as playing a more vital role than simply conveying ideas about intrapsychic processes. They considered communication as a means of change.

Table 1.1 depicts the main differences between the MRI brief strategic model and the traditional analytic therapies of the time.

Table 1.1 The traditional approach and the MRI strategic model

TRADITIONAL THERAPY	MRI STRATEGIC MODEL
Focus on interpreting, explaining and insight	Focus on changing the present complaint
Focus on the past	Focus on the present
Pathologizing perspective	Non-pathologizing perspective
Focus on theory	Focus on action
Problems exist within individuals (intrapsychic origins)	Problems are the result of interactions (social origins)
Change requires years. Therapy is long-term by design	Change can be achieved in a brief period. Therapy is brief by design
Fixed weekly sessions	Flexible schedule of sessions
Acceptance of one fixed reality	Acceptance of multiple views of reality
Communication as conduit of information	Communication as a conduit of change
Adherence to theory	Adherence to client's goal

What's in the word 'strategic'?

The MRI brief model is often dubbed as interactional therapy or problem-solving brief therapy. It is, however, mostly referred to as a strategic approach to therapy. The term 'strategic' is used to denote the therapist's initiative to develop a strategy or intervention to change the behaviour of clients toward their problems and then convince them to implement it (Weakland et al. 1974/2011). Haley actually coined the term 'strategic' (Haley 1973, Haley and Richeport-Haley 2003) but he broke away from the MRI group and developed a strategic family approach that also dealt with hierarchy and family structure. As a result, he distanced himself from the MRI model, which focused on how clients are interacting to solve their problems without assigning further meaning to their behaviour (Quick 2008).

Due to its sometimes unorthodox directives and homework assignments, as well as the importance placed on active therapist involvement, strategic therapy was criticized for being overly controlling, manipulative and even unethical in its practice. However, the mindset of the approach had not been fully understood. It is true that the strategic process, being directive, places the therapist in an active role and that therapist involvement is very important (Coyne and Pepper 1998). This is because strategic therapists believe that clients seek to be influenced in order to reduce distress and change. They also believe that influence is inherent in every communication and that there is no such thing as an influence-free conversation (Watzlawick et al. 1967/2011). They are concerned that, without plan development and a commitment to action, therapy will be reduced to a mere conversation that will not serve the client's needs. Strategic therapists were also accused of not paying due attention to creating a strong, positive relationship with the client. However, the implementation of therapist directives and tasks makes an effective therapeutic alliance a necessary factor for success (Rohrbaugh and Shoham 2015).

Finally, another popular misconception has been the idea that the strategic approach is completely devoid of reflection and insight. It is true that strategic theorists do not embrace knowing 'why' as a precondition for change. However, new insights often occur during or following homework assignments and directives. They come about during the process of change or as a result of it (Duncan and Solovey 1989). Thus, self-awareness may not be a precondition for change but it is often a post-condition of it.

Brief strategic and other approaches

The Mental Research Institute is considered the birthplace of systemic, family and brief approaches to therapy (Nichols and Schwartz 2005). This is why you will detect similarities between the MRI strategic theory with action inquiry, action learning, cognitive approaches, the narrative approach, single-session therapy and the solution-focused model.

Action inquiry delivers an analysis of the situation, engages a group of participants from across various departments that draws upon different perspectives, promotes a process of reflection and creates new ideas to be put into practice and evaluated (Torbert and Associates 2004). It is similar to the strategic approach as it is present focused, goal driven and action orientated. The same holds true for the action learning model of problem-solving, which is also concerned with a situational analysis. It notices the gap between where we are currently and where we want to go, followed by the negotiation and implementation of a solution (Pedler 2011). Additionally, action learning's concept of single- and double-loop learning is similar to the notion of first- and second-order changes in the strategic approach. In single-loop learning, we fix errors in what we are doing and proceed to do it better, whereas double-loop learning entails challenging thinking habits and acting in new ways (Argyris and Schön 1978, Sandars 2006, Volz-Peacock et al. 2016).

Despite the commonalities, the MRI strategic approach is less concerned about situation analysis and more interested in the assessment of attempted solutions. Although there is a problem analysis in the first step, it is applied for the purpose of using that information to review and change ongoing ineffective attempts at a solution. Action learning talks about three types of problems (Pedler 2011), whereas the strategic approach highlights three types of solutions, which will be described in the following chapters (Watzlawick et al. 1974/2011). Finally, cognitive restructuring focuses on ideational content and change and is a central component of the cognitive approach (Clark 2013). Although the strategic approach assesses and changes the client's perceptions, it has a specific intention – to introduce new solutions that will interrupt the cycle of problem-maintenance behaviour.

Narrative therapy and subsequently narrative coaching help clients create change by re-authoring their life stories (White and Epston 1990). Change occurs by expanding on problem-free instances, referred to as unique outcomes or innovative moments, akin to the exceptions utilized in the solution-focused approach (Gonçalves et al. 2009, White and Epston 1990). Both strategic and narrative approaches are non-pathologizing models. They view clients as separate from their problems, utilize homework tasks and share the importance of language in change conversations (Carr 1998, Jensen et al. 2018). However, while narrative professionals identify themselves as non-directive, strategic coaches dismiss the idea that one can truly be non-directive. The narrative focus is on meaning-making and constructing alternative realities instead of on problem-solving (Stelter 2013). Constructing stories rather than disrupting them, as well as identifying a major thread in the client's life which obstructs the desired direction, underlies the narrative effort (Stelter and Law 2010). On the other hand, the core of the strategic approach is to identify a major thread of problematic attempted solution strategies, disrupt maladaptive solution patterns and then construct new ones.

Single-session therapy and single-session coaching (Dryden 2019), a recent evolution of the strategic approach (Perrotta 2020), share the premise that positive change need not be dependent on long-term intervention (Fullen 2019). Just like the MRI strategic approach, the single-session model is brief by design, with the belief that one session could be all that is needed without necessarily being limited to only one session (Dryden 2020). It is goal directed, focused on the present and shares strategic strategies (see Chapter 3) such as seeding, changing perceptions and actions, going slow and matching the client's worldview (Rosenbaum et al. 1990, Amini and Woolley 2011, Hoyt and Talmon, 2014, Dryden 2019). Despite the common ground, it does not share the distinctive focus of the MRI strategic model, which centres on identifying and breaking dysfunctional solution patterns.

John Weakland was a mentor to Insoo Kim Berg, who studied at the MRI. He also happened to be a mentor to Steve de Shazer and introduced them to each other at an MRI conference. They started a variation of MRI strategic therapy that came to be known as the solution-focused approach (Quick 2008, Visser 2013). As a spin-off of the original strategic perspective, it comes as no surprise that the two approaches have much in common, to the extent that they are often thought identical. They are present focused, goal driven and action orientated, with the aim of resolving clients' current complaints as briefly as possible (Fisch et al. 1982, Bannink and Jackson 2011, Visser 2013). Both take their non-pathological perspectives seriously, lacking extensive diagnoses while being pragmatic and committed to results.

However, de Shazer departed from the strategic model and shifted the emphasis of the MRI model. The solution-focused approach creates solutions by focusing on the exceptions to the problem *independently of how it is formed and maintained* (Nardone and Portelli 2005). In contrast to the MRI strategic model, recognizing how the problem is maintained is not considered necessary and therefore neither is a detailed analysis of the complaint nor the client's attempted solutions. What does matter is identifying when the problem is absent (exceptions), attending to the client's behaviour during those exceptions and encouraging them to do more of what works. The most fundamental difference between the MRI strategic and solution-focused approach is related to the concept of solution (Shoham et al. 1995, Priest and Gass 1997).

The brief strategic approach attends to the client's attempted solutions that are perpetuating or aggravating the problem. The aim is to promote less of the same ineffective patterns and eventually to implement new solution patterns that are usually very different from the original ones, as we'll see in the next chapters. The solution-focused model, on the other hand, emphasizes identifying exceptions to the problem upon which new solutions are promoted and amplified. Have these two approaches become so conflicting that we need to choose one or the other? Quick (1994) suggests that a blended approach offers added benefits. After all, the brief strategic model is process based rather than theoretically based. Being relatively devoid of binding theoretical content, it does not exclude other approaches (Held 1986, Soo-Hoo 1997), particularly when it comes to problem resolution and helping clients get unstuck.

In light of MRI's influence, one would expect a larger pool of existing research on brief strategic applications. It is possible that, because of the controversies that ensued and the fact that MRI researchers did not have a reputation for diplomacy and thus did not engage in semantics, the bulk of research was directed to its solution-focused 'offspring'. Nevertheless, despite the need for more research, the brief strategic approach has withstood the test of time and has demonstrated effectiveness across a wide range of problems (Chubb 1982, Eisenberg and Wahrman 1994, Caniato and Skorjanec 2002, Hale and Frusha 2016, Rakowska 2015, Pietrabissa et al. 2017, Hoyt 2019).

Outcome studies have shown high satisfaction and resolution rates with lasting results and low levels of relapse. Gains achieved with the brief strategic approach appear to be more successfully sustained over time than gains from other interventions such as emotion-focused or cognitive-behavioural (Rohrbaugh and Shoham 2001, Castelnuovo et al. 2011, Pietrabissa et al. 2017). A promising initiative is SYPRENE (Vitry et al. 2020), a newly established international 'SYstemic Practice REsearch NEtwork' that aims to focus on the effectiveness and efficiency of strategic therapy. However, as you have probably noticed, the interest lies primarily in therapeutic applications. Hopefully, this book will spark an interest in researching brief strategic outcomes in coaching contexts.

Over the years, a range of psychological approaches and therapeutic techniques have been adapted for coaching contexts (Whybrow and Palmer 2006) and are commonly practised by coaching professionals. The brief strategic process is based on the central MRI concept that problems are maintained by the way we interact with them (Watzlawick et al. 1974/2011, Fisch et al. 1982, Weakland and Fisch 2010, Armatas 2019). The next chapter explains the attempted solutions theory – the logic upon which the brief strategic approach was developed. It discusses how problems are formed and maintained over time by our very attempts to solve them. Chapter 3 introduces common strategic strategies used to enhance the prospects of goal success before moving on to the actual brief strategic process of change.

The strategic process has been broken down into three stages. Chapter 4 covers the first stage – referred to as the clarification stage – during which the problem is defined, the desired goal clarified and the first minimal steps set. Chapter 5 describes the exploration stage, which is the second part of the strategic process. It involves investigating and assessing attempted solutions to determine which maladaptive ones are creating and maintaining the problem. Chapter 6 discusses the final action stage, during which vastly different new solutions are introduced and implemented by the coachee in order to create the desired change. Strategic case-related dialogues are depicted in Chapter 8 to aid with the application of the model and how it is put into practice. The final chapter offers food for thought and encourages strategic reflection – could we, in our attempts to help our clients or employees, inadvertently become part of the problem?

The proposed brief strategic process is based on the central MRI concept that problems are being maintained by the way we interact with them (Watzlawick et al. 1974/2011, Fisch et al. 1982, Weakland and Fisch 2010, Armatas 2019). The idea that our attempted solutions are the problem – rather than the problem *per se* – is known as the attempted solutions theory.

2 The Problem Lies in the Solution: The Attempted Solutions Theory

In his book *The Road Less Travelled*, Scott Peck (2012) opted to start the first chapter with three words: life is difficult. And, at times, it certainly can be. There is no shortage of difficulties that come our way but also no shortage of attempted solutions to get them out of our way. Before exploring the attempted solutions concept in detail, it is necessary to mention that, strategically speaking, 'difficulties' and 'problems' do not share the same meaning. Difficulties are common, undesirable life circumstances we cope with every day and may resolve on their own. If they persist and we do not have an available solution, and they are not too much of a hassle we may decide to live with them, at least until we revisit our initial decision and decide to act instead. Most of our difficulties can be resolved by taking simple logical measures without the need for special problem-solving. But not all. When our common-sense solutions do not work and our continual efforts bring no results, we reach a 'deadlock' (Watzlawick et al. 1974/2011). It is then that we speak of 'problems'.

The attempted solutions theory is the cornerstone of the brief strategic approach. It offers an explanation for how problems are formed and maintained over time, with the central idea being that problems are created, maintained or worsened by our very attempts to solve them. The concept asserts two conditions as being required for problem development: 1) the difficulty being mishandled, which refers to choosing the wrong solution, and 2) applying more of the same ineffective solution when the difficulty is not resolved (Watzlawick et al. 1974/2011, Fisch et al. 1982).

Three types of maladaptive solutions

Tackling difficulties involves devising and selecting solutions (Fisch et al. 1982) but, despite our best intentions, our tactics may complicate rather than resolve our difficulties. In an attempt to cope with our troubles, we may mishandle the situation by applying any of the following three types of misguided solutions (Fraser 1995, Watzlawick et al. 1974/2011):

1 Not taking action when action is necessary.
2 Taking action when we should not.
3 Taking the wrong action.

Action is not taken when action is necessary

One way of (mis)handling a difficulty is by not acting when an action is required. Wishful thinking, a form of passive coping, delays actively addressing an unpleasant situation. Comforting beliefs in the face of an unwanted reality tend to replace distress. Hoping that the issue will resolve itself, even when the facts show otherwise, is a typical example (Georgiou and Fotiou 2019, Pimentel and Cravo 2013, Sigall et al. 2000). Denial is its closest relative and a popular coping solution most of us have at some point practised. Denial can take various forms: minimizing the potential impact of the situation, denying responsibility through blaming or outright denial of the existence of any difficulty. Although denial may be initially beneficial, as it allows time to process upsetting information, the situation remains unresolved and it will have to be tackled at some point. When that point comes, it is likely that the difficulty has been compounded. Needless to say, both coping strategies stall required action.

Action is taken when it should not be

A second misguided attempted solution is trying to a) change a difficulty that is essentially unchangeable, in which case acceptance would be a more effective alternative, or b) attempting to solve a 'problem' that is non-existent. Eager to avoid a potential hardship, we often intervene too soon and unnecessarily complicate matters. Let me share a personal story. Not long ago, I had finished conducting a workshop and was flying back home. I had fallen asleep soon after take-off but my nap was abruptly interrupted by severe turbulence. The crying and panicked shrieks of fellow passengers were a testament to the seriousness of the situation. Luckily, the threat was short-lived but the experience was not; emotions tend to linger longer than the actual events.

Not far behind me, a woman in her mid-fifties was noticeably distraught. As I questioned my first impulse to jump in and help, I observed a group of young women consoling her. They were doing a stellar job of both comforting and allowing her to safely express her emotions. So, I opted to engage in watchful waiting instead. I slipped a note to the flight attendant stating that I'm a psychologist and available to assist if needed but for the time being all gestures to help were actually helpful. Eventually, the genuine care of fellow passengers bore positive results.

What if I acted on my initial impulse to intervene while she was already being helped? An unnecessary intervention could have changed the course of what was already working – and not in a good way. The underlying message of my involvement would have most likely been read as, *'the support you are receiving is not enough, you need more than that'*, implying *'you're not doing that well'*, which understandably could have led to an intensification of emotions. My well-intentioned expert intervention could have shifted her sense of self from being simply a frightened passenger to a traumatized one in need of additional help.

The wrong action is taken

When we are in a hard place, our instinctive response is to do something about it. Yet taking action when action is needed doesn't guarantee favourable results. Unintended consequences develop when the wrong action is taken. A sequence of events unfolds when we pursue change. It includes a difficulty or unsatisfactory situation that needs to change, a desired goal that craves fulfilment, a chosen solution as the means of attaining the desired goal and, finally, the outcome. The outcome relies on the selected solution. This is illustrated in Figure 2.1.

Consider the manager who attempts to improve a team's subpar performance through micromanagement (Armatas 2019). Contrary to the manager's intentions, the solution of increasingly directing and controlling employees strips away their motivation, commitment and productivity (Serrat 2017). In this example, illustrated in Figure 2.2, the team's performance is the target of change and the manager's goal is to improve the bottom line. The action taken to accomplish the goal is to exercise a higher dose of control and the by-product of the faulty attempted solution is an unanticipated performance slump.

Figure 2.1 The change pursuit sequence

Figure 2.2 Example of wrong action taken

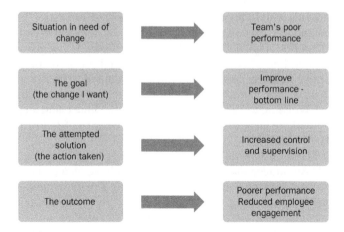

Taking action at the wrong level is the most common category of mishandling difficulties (Fraser 1995) and the one coaches encounter most often in their work.

The attempted solutions theory and the process of problem formation

In most cases, our difficulties respond positively to what common sense dictates. On occasion, common sense proves to be bad sense and acting logically, as illogical as it may sound, becomes the key ingredient of trouble. The longer we are stuck with an unresolved problem, the more likely we are to be stuck in a pattern where the 'remedy' has backfired. The solution we relied upon to set us free has entrapped us in a problem-maintaining vicious cycle where more of our same ineffective solutions leads to an impasse (Watzlawick et al. 1974/2011, Weakland et al. 1974).

As illustrated in Figure 2.3, the possibility of falling prey to the vicious cycle of problem-reinforcing solutions starts the moment we decide to tackle a difficulty. It's important that we don't turn our attention solely on ourselves. Family, friends and co-workers often come to us with their own bag of attempted solutions in an effort to offer assistance that inadvertently contributes to the problem. Social context and interactions are of paramount importance in brief strategic coaching and should always be taken into account. The following sequence describes how our efforts to cope with a difficulty eventually turns it into a larger-scale problem (Watzlawick et al. 1974/2011, Chubb 1982, Fisch et al. 1982):

1   A difficulty arises and we decide to resolve it.
2   We have a certain perception about how that difficulty originated and what needs to be done to moderate or eliminate it.
3   We select what seems to be the most logical and fitting solution in line with our view of the problem.
4   We put our strategy to the test and expect our attempted solution to bring the desired results.
5   If our attempted solution proves to be the right choice, we can happily go about our business with one more success story under our belts.
6   If not, we reapply the solution that should logically have worked in the first place. We succumb to a 'do more of the same' mindset.
7   The difficulty persists or takes a turn for the worse. In some cases, new difficulties emerge as a result of our mishandling.
8   Driven with a mindset of not giving up, we insist on doing more of the same and get caught up in a vicious cycle of problem maintenance. The initial difficulty eventually progresses into a full-blown problem.

Figure 2.3 The vicious cycle of problem maintenance

Why do we stick to solutions that don't work? We resort to the solutions that make the most sense to us, following the assumption that if it's reasonable then it must be correct, even when the evidence shows otherwise. What would be more logical for Hercules, in his battle against the nine-headed Lernaean Hydra, than to decapitate? That's what he did, only to soon discover that, for each severed head, two more vicious ones appeared. If he persisted with the logical solution, semi-god or not, it would have led to his demise (Armatas 2020).

Our behaviours are usually driven by what seems rational or logical rather than what works. For instance, it is logical to tell a frustrated person to calm down even though it usually has the reverse effect. Yet, when our suggestion adds fuel to the fire, we continue to respond with more calming advice. The more we persist with our logical response, the more the anger escalates until the situation gets out of hand. It is this action–reaction pattern (Nardone 2005) that strategic coaches aim to change.

Watzlawick (1988) mentions two logical traps that drive maladaptive solutions. First, he draws attention to the danger of 'twice as much is twice as good' (1988: 26). This refers to the assumption that, if a solution has been effectively applied in one area, it can be equally applied to more and more problems. However, what proved to be successful in one place could be detrimental in another. In reality, a higher dose of an otherwise effective behaviour may null its effectiveness even in the same situation. Take overpreparation, for example. Preparing a speech or practising the guitar before a special performance can make the difference between mediocrity and mastery. Over-rehearsing, on the other hand, can see your hard-earned gains suffer.

The second fallacy about change is the assumption that if something is bad, then the opposite must be good. When employees are given free rein at work and do not deliver, strict control may take its place. When politeness attracts disrespect, bullying may be the alternative. As you will soon notice, in some cases going the opposite way is the correct way to go. The problem lies in believing that such a turn in behaviour is necessary to achieve resolution, which doesn't leave much room for deliberation before acting. In strategic terms, deliberating means focusing on and implementing what works, not what seems rational or feels right.

Focusing on how problems are maintained

Strategic thinking differs from the traditional view that change occurs when we become more aware of our ineffective behaviours and by understanding how we came to be a certain way. Rather than relying on awareness alone, the brief strategic coach provides opportunities to practise new ways of behaving and thinking (Andreas 1991). Awareness is not considered a change agent unless it is acted upon and strategic coaches encourage action. Since aetiology resides in our maladaptive solutions, attending to the coachee's past, looking for underlying causes of behaviour, understanding intrapsychic experiences and exploring why something happens is neither a priority nor a necessity. Instead, the primary interest lies in exploring attempted solutions and how problems are maintained (Watzlawick et al. 1974/2011, Duncan et al. 1990, Soo-Hoo 1997, Rohrbaugh and Shoham 2001).

This should not be taken as discrediting the general benefits of insight. It is mostly a case of denouncing the traditional assumption that insight and change are interdependent and that the former is an essential requirement for the latter. In strategic thinking, change is more likely to contribute to insight than the other way round (Erickson and Rossi 1979, Gordon and Meyers-Anderson 1981, Andreas 1991). Insight and even emotional release can accompany change but it is not a necessary factor for change to occur. Consider your clientele. Is every coachee who has consulted you lacking in insight? Are all your clients unaware of how their prior experiences have influenced their current situation? Some may have already gone through a process of inner work and, despite their strides in self-awareness, the problem remains unaltered. On the other end of the spectrum, you may have clients who have successfully reached problem resolution and come to new realizations as a result of their success.

MRI strategic coaches do not explore whether people's misguided solution attempts harbour secondary gains or other interior motives. They regard coachees as acting in a certain way because the coachees genuinely believe they have found the most effective tactic that will bring the most benefit. As we have discussed, the more logical their solution strategy appears, the more effective they will expect it to be. Hence, it is positive intentions that fuel solution attempts, even when they prove to be unhelpful. The belief that positive intentions drive our actions governs strategic work and strengthens the conviction that exploring underlying motivations, resistance or other determinants of behaviour is unnecessary for successful problem resolution (Andreas 1991, Havens 2003).

Consider a writer who is experiencing a significant slowdown in creative work due to writer's block and has a deadline looming. Rather than concentrating on the problem *per se*, a strategic approach will focus on *how the writer has been trying to handle the 'block'*. The emphasis will be on past and current solution attempts; what the writer and other parties involved have been persistently doing or not doing to control, minimize or eliminate the problem (Soo-Hoo 1997, Quick 2008, Armatas 2010, Weakland and Fisch 2010). By following this typical strategic line of inquiry, an answer to the all-important 'why' will be revealed. It is just that, in brief strategic coaching, the 'why' lies in the misguided solution attempts, not deep within. It may be revealed that the attempted solution that has been reinforcing the writer's block involves reading articles online on how to overcome writer's block!

Examples of attempted solutions gone wrong

Everyday examples of both individual and organizational faulty solutions abound. In Israel, a group of daycare centres decided to deal with parents being late to pick up their children, forcing teachers to stay after closing time. Their solution attempt was to introduce a monetary fine for those who failed to show up on time. The result was not what they expected. There was in fact a rise in the number of late-coming parents and an increase in the overall delay time. Why? The answer lies in the solution. The fine was less that what parents would normally pay for babysitting so the delay was a sensible financial decision. As it turned out, this was a bargain compared to standard hourly rates they would pay elsewhere (Gneezy and Rustichini 2000). To make matters worse, the number of late-coming parents remained higher than before the intervention even after the fine was withdrawn.

The following sneak peeks of solution attempts often complicate the problem. It does not mean that these solution strategies will certainly backfire. In some cases, they may work but, more often than not, they tend to maintain the problem, aggravate it or even create further difficulties (Watzlawick et al. 1974/2011, Fisch et al. 1982, Coyne and Pepper 1998, Rohrbaugh and Shoham 2001, Hart and Randell 2006, Rohrbaugh and Shoham 2015). Examples are when:

- attempting to cheer up someone who feels depressed adds to the depression
- certain thoughts return with a vengeance after attempting to suppress them in hopes of strengthening mental control. The same holds true when trying to control emotions by withholding them; they resurge more powerfully than before

- attempting assurances and explanations to assuage a partner's suspicions of infidelity or betrayal serve only to strengthen the partner's suspicions
- a company trying to protect employees' emotional state by withholding information about a traumatic event at work damages the trust it has worked hard to build
- trying to force something to happen that usually occurs spontaneously stops it from occurring altogether
- trying to reach an accord through opposition leads to discord
- avoiding a feared event to ease discomfort turns the fear into a phobia
- attempting to increase confidence through reassurances ends up increasing self-doubt and reliance on external validation
- trying to reduce anxiety by reading about anxiety online has the opposite effect
- trying to empower employees by assigning them more tasks of increasing complexity leaves them overworked, stressed and unhappy.

Additional examples of maladaptive solutions are also encountered when trying to decrease something makes you increase it or vice versa, when trying to remember something makes you forget it and trying to forget it makes you remember, when pursuing leads to distancing, when pushing for change makes the other person support the status quo more intensely, or when building a positive working alliance with your coachees at work undermines the 'authority' of, and confidence in, their manager (Rohrbaugh and Shoham 2001: 7). See Table 2.1 for more examples.

Table 2.1 Examples of attempted solutions that perpetuate or compound the problem

DIFFICULTY	GOAL	ATTEMPTED SOLUTION
Conflicts	Improve communication/relationships	• Avoiding conflict/placating • Psychoanalysing the tension • Calming down suggestions • Directives to get along and be agreeable • Responding aggressively • Becoming apologetic/defensive
Performance slump/unsatisfactory results	Enhanced performance	• Increasing performance appraisals • Criticizing • Instilling a sense of urgency/threat • Increasing control tactics • Overthinking before acting • Overpreparation or over-rehearsing • Comparison with others

DIFFICULTY	GOAL	ATTEMPTED SOLUTION
Low morale and motivation/low confidence	Empowerment	• Pep-talk and efforts to enthuse where morale is low • Offering additional choices to those who are overwhelmed and highly stressed • Painting an overly bright future too soon • Seeking confidence through frequent reassurance or overpreparation • Excessive encouragement, support and praise • Too much independence (leaving them feeling unsupported)
Lack of innovation	Creativity	• Forcing creativity by rewarding it or penalizing its absence • Intentional innovation • Increased performance reviews to encourage creativity

Adapted from author's own work as previously published in *The Practitioner's Handbook of Team Coaching* (Routledge, 2019)

Solutions create problems

The MRI brief strategic view focuses on the idea that our attempts to change, control, prevent or eliminate difficulties often cause a vicious circle of problem persistence. It's best reflected in the phrase 'the problem lies in the solution'. The solutions we pick perpetuate or complicate the very problems we are trying to resolve (Watzlawick et al. 1974/2011, Watzlawick and Coyne 1980, Fisch et al. 1982, Fisch and Schlanger 1999, Weakland and Fisch 2010, Watzlawick et al. 1967/2011, Quick 2012, Armatas 2019). Hence, the focus is on a client's solution attempts rather than on the problem. The assumption is that the client has been attempting to change the existing difficulty but going about it the wrong way. Dealing with how the client has been trying to cope with the problem is more important than dealing with the problem itself. For example, if a coachee's presenting problem is their conflict with a partner, the focus will be on how the client has been trying to solve the issue. What has the coachee been doing to stop conflict from escalating? To a strategic coach, where there's a problem, there's a misguided solution (Segal 1991).

The 'attempted solutions theory' does not stop at identifying clients' resolution efforts. That is just one part of the process. When solution strategies have been identified, the next step will be to replace them with different tactics to break the vicious circle between attempted solutions and persistence of the problem (Rohrbaugh and Shoham 2001). How is the 'the more I try, the worse it gets' pattern interrupted? The strategic process of breaking the faulty solution pattern involves the following steps:

1 defining the problem and clarifying the goal
2 exploring attempted solutions
3 developing and implementing new solution.

Obviously, no change will occur unless the coachee is convinced to try the new suggested behaviour. Because the new solution is often in a different direction to the previous one, it may seem counterintuitive or even risky to give it a go. Therefore, in addition to building a strong working alliance, the brief strategic model utilizes several strategies that aim to convince the coachee to try a different solution approach and feel at ease with its implementation. The following chapter explores these strategies.

3   Brief Strategic Coaching: Common Strategies

Change, as desirable as it may be, remains unfamiliar territory and unfamiliarity begets anxiety. Moreover, change may lead to gains but there is also a loss involved since it entails giving up or at least modifying old familiar ways. In brief strategic coaching, client hesitancy may be more pronounced than in other approaches because it directs coachees in a direction that is often counterintuitive to them. The strategies described in this chapter prepare a better reception of proposed new behaviours and solutions while maintaining a positive working alliance. They set the stage for an agreement to test the proposed behaviour before the intervention is directly introduced, in order to enhance the prospects of goal success. The most common strategies utilized are:

- reframing
- seeding
- pre-empting
- paradox
- matching client's language
- implications and presuppositions
- manoeuvrability: keeping options open
- behavioural assignments.

Reframing

Asking coachees to depart from previous efforts, especially when our suggestions seem to move them away from their goal rather towards it, requires attentive handling. The more radical the departure, the more they will cling to their familiar attempted solutions (Fisch and Schlanger 1999). There is a risk related to requesting coachees to stop their solutions, despite their ineffectiveness. They are likely to think: 'I've been trying so hard to deal with this and it didn't amount to much, so I don't want to imagine what might happen if I stop!' Consider telling exhausted parents *not* to convey the message 'You must do your homework' or 'Do your chores' to their children who have already been neglecting their responsibilities. The parents may tentatively agree to give it a try but not before conjuring up images of havoc at home. Reframing is a strategy enlisted to secure client consensus and encourage coachees to test unchartered waters, and it has a special place in strategic coaching.

Reframing helps coachees by shifting their frame of reference from 'what's logical' to 'what works' (Fisch and Schlanger 1999). This is a critical strategic objective, since this different a conceptualization leads to a different solution (Goldenberg et al. 2016). Any approach that encourages the coachee to gain a different perspective on the problem in a way that facilitates the implementation of appropriate new solutions involves reframing (Watzlawick et al. 1974/2011: 93, Soo-Hoo 1997, Horigian et al. 2004, Yapko 2015, Goldenberg et al. 2016, Armatas 2019). Reframing can be described as changing the viewpoint from which a situation is experienced and placing it in another frame which fits the facts of the same situation equally well or even better, thereby changing its entire meaning. It is important to emphasize that, when reframing, the situation remains unchanged. What does change is the meaning attributed to the situation.

Most of us have used reframing casually in our daily lives. How often have we said to someone – or have been told ourselves – 'Why don't you look at this in a different way?' (Yapko 2015)? That's a reframe. Another example would be when you're feeling just fine at work until someone asks, 'Are you OK? You don't look so good!' – and fine is no longer how you feel. This shows that reframing is not limited to a change in our perception of a problem but also a change in how we view ourselves, others and the world. You can reframe a positive situation into a negative one and a negative one into a positive. What is viewed as useful can be re-evaluated as disadvantageous, as in the case of attempted solutions. What is perceived as bad can be reconsidered as having positive attributes, such as when a behaviour that may cause problems in one area is regarded as an asset elsewhere. For example, a person who may have been labelled immature and considered a liability at work could also be perceived, for the very same reason, as a person who celebrates life. What is impoverishing one area is enriching another. Reframing can be implemented in two ways: reframing the problem situation and reframing the solution.

Reframing the problem situation

Reframing is often selected as a strategy to redefine the problem to make it easier to resolve (Haley 1976, Mattila 2001). Framing the presenting complaint in a new way renders the problem more manageable and lightens the load by reducing the intensity of associated emotions. It further enhances client motivation and facilitates mobilization towards the desired goal (Carratala et al. 2016). The coach listens to the client's choice of words and reframes them by restating their words with what seems to be slight changes. Impulsive becomes spontaneous, rebellious becomes courageous, stress is reflected back as 'really wanting things to work out', fear becomes overly cautious and stubbornness is offered as determination. A popular case of reframing, illustrated in the following dialogue, is led by Virginia Satir about a father who saw fault in his daughter's stubbornness (Grinder and Bandler 1982: 8–9):

Satir: *You're a man who has gotten ahead in your life. Is this true?*

Father: Yes.

Satir: *Was all that you have, just given to you? Did your father own the bank and just say 'Here, you are president of the bank'?*

Father: No, no. I worked my way up.

Satir: *So, you have some tenacity, don't you?*

Father: Yes.

Satir: *Well, there is a part of you that has allowed you to be able to get where you are, and to be a good banker. And sometimes you have to refuse people things that you would like to be able to give them, because you know if you did, something bad would happen later on.*

Father: Yes.

Satir: *Well, there is a part of you that's been stubborn enough to really protect yourself in very important ways.*

Father: Well, yes. But, you know, you can't let this kind of thing get out of control.

Satir: *Now, I want you to turn and look at your daughter, and to realize beyond a doubt that you've taught her how to be stubborn and how to stand up for herself, and that that is something priceless. This gift that you've given her is something that can't be bought, and it's something that may save her life. Imagine how valuable that will be when your daughter goes out on a date with a man who has bad intentions.*

In the above exchange, the situation which, according to banker-dad, was a nasty case of stubbornness remains unchanged. What changed was the meaning attached to stubbornness. It was no longer just a problem. It was repackaged and presented as an asset for the daughter and an achievement for the father. A closer look at the dialogue reveals that Satir did not just blurt out a new meaning. She did not rush into handing him a new outlook. She carefully selected questions that drew the dad's attention to his own stubbornness, also referred to as tenacity, and to the benefits he reaped as a result.

It's essential to refrain from any attempt to reframe until the coachee has been heard, acknowledged and given adequate time to describe the problem in detail. Consider a coachee whose presenting complaint concerns a team manager being overly critical and controlling. Any premature reframing of the behaviour with a positive connotation will trigger an array of negative feelings, including anger and resentment. However, when done respectfully and in a timely fashion, one can plant the reframing seeds early on, in the problem definition stage, and capitalize on them later (see *Seeding* below). This common practice is depicted in the following conversation with Tracy who, unlike the rest of her team, is overworked and feels unfairly treated.

Coach: *I see, so it's not uncommon for your boss to give you last-minute work, just before you're about to call it a day?*
Tracy: No, it has become very common.
Coach: *What about the rest of the staff?*
Tracy: What about them?
Coach: *Are they putting in long hours too?*
Tracy: No and that's what infuriates me. It's always me.
Coach: *I see, seems logical to feel the way you feel. Do you always deliver?*
Tracy: Always.
Coach: *To a high standard?*
Tracy: Yes.
Coach: *So, he knows he can rely on you to do the work? Correct me if I'm wrong.*
Tracy: No, you're not. That's how it is.
Coach: *And not only do the work but do it well.*
Tracy: Yes.
Coach: *That's safe, isn't it?*
Tracy: What?
Coach: *Knowing he can delegate work at the last minute and regardless of how you feel and how tired you are, you will do a good job ... that will give any leader peace of mind! Wouldn't it?*
Tracy: It would, but who's going to give me some peace of mind?
Coach: *Now that's work you've given yourself this time, isn't it?*
Tracy: It is (laughs).
Coach: *And you know how to deliver, don't you?*
Tracy: Yes.
Coach: *So, when he relies on you at the very last minute, how do you usually respond?*

Two reframes take place in this dialogue. Delivering good-quality work is addressed as a resource Tracey can rely on this time to deliver the goods to herself. And the last sentence is the start of the second reframe before exploring her attempted solutions. Her employer's behaviour is referred to as *relying on her* as a way to soften the emotional intensity of the situation. This facilitates moving away from a 'stop picking on me or exploiting me' stance to a 'sorry but you just can't solely rely on me anymore' message. Reframing how one looks at the problem leads to changes in how one tries to resolve it. This brings us to reframing the solution.

Reframing the solution

Let's assume that the situation has been reframed through carefully selected questions, comments and redescriptions that allow the coachee's initial viewpoint to be modified. The next step is to suggest or co-design a new solution tactic. Simply proposing a new solution, especially if it is drastically different to what has been employed, may be insufficient to mobilize the coachee into action. Just like reframing the problem, it is crucial to reframe the solution in terms that the coachee understands. Establishing a reframe that is compatible with the coachee's language and views will enhance receptivity (Fisch and Schlanger 1999). To the person who values creativity, the suggestion is framed as creative; to the rebellious, it can be unconventional; to the coachee who values a challenge, the suggestion is framed as an unusual way to approach the problem – and to the coachee who values stretch goals, the suggestion is framed as challenging (Mattila 2001).

Consider David, who has shown up for coaching to improve his interpersonal skills. He is not against the idea of coaching but the presenting complaint is not aligned with his manager's. He emphatically tells the coach that it is not a matter of interpersonal skills and that the real problem is that he is stuck with a bunch of idiots. The presenting complaint that David is ready to work on is acknowledged and the coaching starts from what he brings to the table.

Coach: *How long have you been with that bunch?* (Although some would reiterate the entire descriptive phrase used, I (the coach) opted not to repeat 'idiots', since the word bunch alone serves as a reflection of his position.)

David: Slightly over a year, although it feels like forever.

Coach: *Well, time goes by much slower when you're not enjoying what you're doing.* (First reframing seeds.) *Did you have similar issues with previous teams?*

David: This is actually the first team I'm leading. And to think I was happy when they announced it to me.

Coach: *You had high hopes ... and the desire to prove to yourself that they were right to invest in you.*

David (Nods.)

Coach: *And then the letdown. Let's return to your disappointment with your team.* (Reframing situation as a disappointment and the 'bunch of idiots' is now referred to as a team.)

David: OK.

Coach: *It just occurred to me ... there's the handling of your team, the handling of your disappointment and the handling of the anxiety to deliver what is expected of you ... am I getting this right?*

David: I didn't think of it that way but yes ...

Coach: *What is most challenging for you – dealing with you team members. the letdown or the anxiety to perform?* (Prioritizing problems, which will be covered in the next chapter.)

David: Honestly, the emotions ...

Coach: *They can be quite intense ... often strong enough to change the way we go about matters.* (Seeding the possibility that he might be contributing to the situation through his behaviour but it is because of emotions not lack of competence.) *How have you gone about coping with the emotions? How have you tried to ease the way you feel?* (Exploring attempted solutions.)

David: Getting the team to deliver. If we start performing as expected, I'll feel much better. (He now calls the 'bunch' a team and uses 'we' for the first time. Meanwhile, he offers an opportunity to reframe the solution as one of improving delivery and offering relief.)

Coach: *I see, it makes sense. Being able to get the team going and meeting expectations will be a big relief wouldn't it? How have you been trying to do that?*

Following further exploration and clarification of past and current efforts to deliver, a new strategy is offered. Reframing the solution as one of positive intention will facilitate trying something different. Maintaining David's initial frame of how to get a bunch of idiots to work harder and smarter while blaming them for poor performance would most likely lead to a deadlock.

Reframing is related to the strategic belief that reality depends on context and reflects social constructions of the world (Segal 1991). As such, there are many versions of reality, some contradictory but all the result of our interaction with others and our conversations with them (Watzlawick 1976, Ray 2018). Strategic professionals respect the client's reality and don't adhere to the idea that the coach has the 'right' mindset and the coachee has the 'wrong' frame of mind. Strategically orientated coaches neither challenge the client's reality nor do they follow a corrective process. They will gently introduce an alternative meaning simply because a new reality will facilitate the coachee's goal attainment. Since, in strategic thinking, reality is invented through communication rather than discovered, communication can also be used to recreate it.

Language can change perceptions and changed perceptions make behavioural change possible. With good reason, paying attention to language is of paramount importance (Watzlawick 1976). Within this context, one can understand the interest placed on moving away from a language based on the premise of an objective reality and towards the use of verbs such as 'it seems' and 'it appears' (Ray 2018). In reflecting the coachee's words, strategic coaches intentionally replace their 'to be' with 'to seem', planting the seeds for alternative meanings to be pursued at a later time.

In short, strategic coaches won't impose their reframe onto their clients. To do so implies that a coach's view or 'reality' is on a higher plane than that of the client. It presumes that a coach's understanding is better than that of their coachees, which goes against the grain of strategic thinking. The reason that a reframe is introduced is simply because the coach believes it is essential for the uptake of the new proposed behaviours that will lead to the desired outcome (Flaskas 1992, Mattila 2001, Goldenberg et al. 2016).

One can think of reframing as a three- step process where the coach:

1   elicits the coachee's frame of reference and meets the coachee where the coachee is
2   acknowledges the coachee's position using the coachee's language; in doing so, the coachee feels understood, valued and respected

3 reframes by introducing alternative meanings that fit the coachee's understanding. When the new meaning is consistent with the coachee's position, it
will make the change more manageable and possibly avoid power struggles
or confrontation with the coach.

Seeding

Seeding is akin to planting seeds in the ground for future harvesting (Short et al.
2005: 101). The strategic coach progressively introduces ideas early in the coaching conversation or in previous sessions. By planting the seeds early, the ground-
work is being made (Haley 1973) so that, when the time comes to introduce the
new idea or behaviour, the coachee responds favourably to what is being suggested (Jacobson 1983). This comes as no surprise, since priming creates a sense
of familiarity with the new information and familiarity increases receptivity.

It would be helpful to think of seeding as dropping hints early in the interaction that allude to a future goal (Zeig 2006a) in order to activate that goal at a
later time (Geary and Zeig 2001). If you are a parent, you may know firsthand
how good your children can be at seeding – unless they're so good at it that you
haven't picked up the clues yet. I might have just spoiled it for the kids, though,
since now you're more than likely to recognize the signs. Zeig (2014) describes
it as analogous to a mystery writer who inserts clues early in the story about
how events will unfold but, unless you're already familiar with how the story
progresses, you don't pick up those clues. It's when you finish the story and
know the finale that you look back and notice all the previous references to the
ending. Just as a writer must know how the story is going to unfold in order to
insert clues early in the book, a coach must have an intention to use a certain
strategy or assign a certain task beforehand in order to employ seeding.

Let's look at this from a coaching perspective. In this example, a strategic
coach intends to use reframing and decides to seed the idea early in the session.
The coachee is sitting in the office, looking at the view from the window. You,
the coach, utilize the moment and mention how you just see the building
across the street but that there's more to what you see, even if you can't see it.
You mention that there's a park nearby:

Coach: *If you look at it from this place here, you can get a glimpse of the
           park.*
Coachee: Oh, yes, I see it.
Coach: *You didn't know you could see it, did you?*
Coachee: No.
Coach: *You just need to look from a different angle and discover there's more
           than one view ... Anyway, back to your goal. We were saying that ...*

After the seeding, you revert back to what you were discussing to avoid further
analysis and to wait until it is time to reap what you've sown.

Pre-empting

The best time to directly introduce a new idea or behaviour is following a successful reframing. As a coach who is using the strategic model, you may want to further reduce client concerns about the new direction you will be proposing. This is done by prefacing the suggestion with remarks that seem to be disqualifying it rather than promoting it. You pre-empt resistance by bringing up the objection you anticipate before the coachee expresses it (Watzlawick et al. 1974/2011, Jacobson 1983). There are many ways to pre-empt before delivering a suggestion with the intent of increasing the chances that it will be acted upon.

Examples of pre-empting phrases are as follows:

- *You will probably find this a bit silly, but I have the impression that ...*
- *This may sound strange, but one could say that ...*
- *I'd like to suggest a solution for this problem, but I am not sure you'll like it ... you might not like it at all in fact, however ...*
- *I know that what I am about to suggest is quite different from what others have suggested and might surprise you, but ...*
- *I know this won't be easy to do, but I am wondering whether ...*
- *Now this may sound counterintuitive or even illogical, but ...*

On a personal note, I recommend following a pre-empting strategy with an explanation of why you are offering the advice that seems counterintuitive. This won't be anything entirely new as you have already seeded or directly highlighted how their logical attempted solutions have complicated their problem. It is, nevertheless, helpful to offer a reminder and paint a clearer picture of why such an apparently illogical direction can actually be the logical way to go. Here's an example:

Coach: *I know this may sound quite counterintuitive, but would you be willing to try something very different? The reason I am suggesting this is that the solutions you've been attempting so far have an underlying message of 'controlling'.*

Coachee: Yes.

Coach: *And the more you have pursued controlling – which is logical – the more the team has been suffering in terms of relationships and productivity. Correct me if I'm wrong.*

Coachee: No, that's right ...

Coach: *In order to get out of that vicious circle, you'll need to move in a different direction. Any idea what that may be?*

Coachee: Give up on controlling...

Coach: *That's spot on. It may have sounded a bit strange before but does it make more sense now?*

Coachee: (Nods.) Yeah ...

Coach: *What would relinquishing control look like?*

Let's revisit David, whom we talked about in relation to reframing, and look at the use of pre-empting in his coaching session:

Coach: *What I am going to tell you is a bit challenging, a bit too challenging for some* (first pre-empting) *but, from what I can tell, you don't seem to shun away from a good challenge, do you?*

David: No.

Coach: *And knowing that the logical solutions that have been applied did not bring the expected results, on the contrary ... I think it would be a clever idea to change direction. Do you think so too?* (David's description of the team as a bunch of idiots implies that he sees himself as an intelligent and competent person.)

David: I guess ...

Coach: *Now this may sound strange at first* (second pre-empting with a presupposition) *but it is quite a clever strategy which I think you'll enjoy toying with ... What do you think of ...?* (Suggestion of new solution is introduced.)

By using pre-empting, you first disqualify the suggestion you will introduce to get the objection out of the way. Then, by explaining the reason for your suggestion, you are sufficiently qualifying it again to secure an agreement from the client to give it a go. Disqualifying it first to reduce hesitancy and positively reframing it later creates a better fit with their new perspective on the situation.

Paradox

With paradox, you propose what you want to discourage – you suggest what the client wants to resolve (Haley 1976, Mozdzierz et al. 1976, West et al. 1986, Nardone and Watzlawick 2005, Weeks 2013). According to Watzlawick (1974/2011), 'be spontaneous' paradoxes are the most prominent types. At some point, most of us have experienced how intending to make or provoke a spontaneous response makes it less likely. Planning spontaneous creativity kills it, willing yourself to fall asleep keeps you awake and trying to control an unwanted thought that keeps popping in your head strengthens it instead. This idea can be flipped to the coachee's benefit with the desired response emerging in reverse. Suggestions of relinquishing control may enhance that control, trying to stay awake may knock you out cold and forgetting about generating original ideas may proliferate them. On a cautionary note, paradoxical interventions should not be attempted when the behaviour suggested involves risks and consequences that are not worth taking (Weeks and L'Abate 1982).

Paradox is often utilized when the presenting complaint is related to what the coachees feel is involuntary behaviour, out of their control, and it is adapted with a particular goal in mind (Haley 1976, Weeks and L'Abate 1982). When you suggest using the very behaviour coachees have been trying to squash, paradoxically they come to realize that they have more control over it than they'd thought. Consider a coachee who is trying to improve their interpersonal relationships but has trouble keeping their anger under control. The suggestion to plan to be angry at a certain time during the day can go two ways. If the client manages to intentionally create the aggravated state, then they can also stop it. If you can increase, you can decrease and you have control back in your hands. If the coachee's efforts fail and their anger diminishes, the perplexed coachee is happy to see that the initial objective is being achieved. It also confirms how the attempted solution of trying to suppress the feeling intensifies the problem and how the client has been contributing to its development. Either way, the coachee benefits.

Coachees are surprised when, instead of eliminating a behaviour, they are advised to perform it; when, instead of relinquishing an unwanted action, they are asked to hold on to it; when, in lieu of concealing a problem, they are advised to advertise it (Watzlawick et al. 1974/2011, Watzlawick 1988). The unexpectedness of a paradoxical suggestion, coupled with the fact that it cannot be resolved by logic, suspends their customary frame of reference and reframing is facilitated (Ruby 2018). Most importantly, clients come to their own conclusions based on their experience of acting out the paradox rather than being told or handed interpretations by the coach.

Remember David's remark about the 'bunch of idiots' he works with? A simple paradox could look like this:

> I would like you to simply be aware of when you are trying to improve your team's results ... And I want you to observe how your team responds to those efforts of yours ... Please do not stop those efforts yet but be more aware of them so that we can have something interesting to talk about next time ... would that be OK?

By telling David not to change anything, we are keeping with his position that others are the problem. His efforts are reframed as efforts to bring results. Observing how others respond to those efforts can get him to think about his own contribution to what happens. If he observes that his behaviour plays an important role in the way the team is working, it is much easier to accept it as a result of 'intending to improve performance' rather than of problems in his behaviour. Finally, adding the word 'yet' to the phrase 'Please don't stop yet' presumes that at some point he will stop.

Here's another example from another scenario:

> I only want you to think about it till our next session. Don't do anything yet. You're a CEO, so the last thing I am going to request from you is to immediately follow along without giving it some thought and coming to your own conclusions about the benefits of changing direction.

The use of paradox has often been criticized as manipulative, disrespectful and dishonest. Strategic professionals disagree. Is it ethical to withhold a strategy that can help to accomplish a desired goal when a coachee is stuck in a problem-reinforcing vicious cycle, especially when other attempted solutions have not worked? Is it ethical to not use a strategy that will facilitate reframing and a change in perspective? Is it more ethical to allow coachees to continue without a solution? (Cade 2013). Is our decision to use or not use a paradox based on the client or on us?

Strategic coaches do not consider a paradox to be dishonest because it is not employed to trick the client and there is no attempt to conceal the intent of the paradoxical suggestion. For example, when suggesting an increase in anxiety to coachees who feel anxious, we are concurrently suggesting that something will happen that may surprise them. We are not hiding the anticipation that there is something to be learned from the unorthodox assignment. Alluding to the benefits of the experiment also offers an additional advantage: that of positive expectancy.

Go slow

One of the most common paradoxical interventions in strategic work is the 'go slow' message (Watzlawick 1974/2011, Fisch et al. 1982, Rohrbaugh and Shoham 2015). Although encouragement and optimism are important components when the first signs of desired change are shared with the coach, there are times when positive reinforcement is not conducive to more change. Although one would expect that reinforcing desired behaviours encourages their recurrence, it may stall change or even reverse it. Encouragement, in this case, becomes the faulty attempted solution and part of the problem. That is why strategic coaches are not known for their cheerleading behaviour. They will validate and compliment the client but at the same time convey a 'go slow' message, cautioning them not to change too quickly as it may be too soon (Quick 2008). Such a move tends to lift the pressure off coachees who feel they have to perform fast and effectively. Moreover, feelings of letting down the coach or themselves are mitigated in case of a less adequate than expected performance. The following is an example of a 'go slow' response after listening to the coachee report that her presentation anxiety hasn't gone away to the extent she had hoped:

> I am actually a bit relieved you still have some of that around ... I am going to ask, if you don't mind, to hold on to some of that stress a bit longer ... Please take your time and don't hurry ...

Brief strategic philosophy embraces the 'go slow to go faster' mindset. As brief strategic coaches actively support the belief that starting small and slow will lead to greater strides, small changes are observed and highlighted (Tomm 1988). Small changes are easier to accomplish and they move coachees away from a sense of urgency which alone can contribute to problem formation and maintenance (Fisch et al. 1982, Rohrbaugh and Shoham 2001). Strategic coaches will not encourage a coachee to pick up the pace as they believe it can serve as an attempted solution which can eventually backfire.

Matching client's language

Another Erickson-inspired practice in brief strategic coaching is matching the client's language. It is the coach who learns to speak the coachee's language rather than the other way round (Watzlawick et al. 1974/2011, Watzlawick 1978). The coach listens closely to the words that reflect the client's motivation, perceptions, values and attitudes (Fölscher-Kingwill and Terblanche 2019). What words do coachees use to describe how they see themselves and other involved parties? In what words do they illustrate their complaint? How do they explain why the problem is happening? How do they portray their theory of why their attempted solutions are not working? (Hart and Randell 2006). The same words are incorporated in the coach's reflections, reframes and suggestions. In addition, language is utilized in a planned manner to reduce the emotional load of a problem. For example, panic may be reflected back as stress, pain as discomfort and fear as insecurity or being overly cautious.

The strategic coach will also use any metaphors the coachee brings to the session. Although an original metaphor can be constructed, there is a preference to work with those found in the coachee's narration (Armatas 2009). Metaphors come with several advantages. They help build rapport, overcome possible resistance to change and test the coachee's response to new ideas. They allow coachees to actively construct for themselves new ways of understanding, while the coach can prepare for future responses and link change to subsequent behaviour (Brown 1997, Queraltó 2006, Armatas 2009, Armatas 2011). Metaphors lend themselves beautifully to reframes. Being attentive to the coachee's words and metaphors will facilitate the framing of suggestions in the language clients already use, understand and follow (Hart and Randell 2006, Watzlawick 1976, Hale and Frusha 2016).

Coachee: It feels like I'm in a pitch-dark tunnel and I can see no way out.

Coach: *We actually had a blackout a couple of nights ago, so I know what you mean. I'm sure you had your share of blackouts where you're in the dark and you can't see a thing.*

Coachee: Sure.

Coach: *It's pitch dark and you need to safely find your way out ... All the way down those stairs... Yes?*

Coachee: Yes.

Coach: *What do you do to find your way out?*

Coachee: I feel my way out.

Coach: *So, you come up with another way, you feel your way out ... Funny that you say that. Remember in our first session, when you told me you're not much a feeling-type of guy?... And yet you feel yourself out* (seeding the idea of unexpected solutions).

Coachee: Hmmm.

Coach: *I actually have an idea that's a bit counterintuitive, but I think this may be a good time to share it with you ...* (Pre-empting and ready to introduce a different strategy.)

Using the coachee's words, phrases and stories is based on Erickson's concept of utilization (Erickson 1959/2009). Utilization is taking everything the client brings to the session and using it to foster change and understanding. Anything, not just words, can be utilized in the session: ideas, achievements, feelings, values, personal events, general events such as storms, earthquakes and even the COVID-related mandatory facemask. A strategic coach is always on the lookout for factors that can help coachees progress towards their goals (Geary 2001).

Implications and presuppositions

Implications and presuppositions are types of indirect suggestions that involve sending a message without actually saying it (Hammond 1990, Marsen 2006).

Presuppositions convey the message that something has happened, is happening or is about to happen (Armatas 2011). Consider these examples:

1 Presume that something is about to happen:

   'I am not sure when the first signs of change will be noticeable but it would help to know what those first signs will be.' (This presupposes that change will happen and it will be noticeable.)

   'Yes, it is logical to find it difficult at first, after all you've been following a certain direction for a long time.' (This presupposes that it will get easier.)

2 Presume that something is happening:

   'That's right, continue relaxing.'

3 Presume that something has already happened:

   'What did you notice happening by going in a different direction?'

Implications are more subtle than presuppositions and they are less likely to be noticed because they are harder to identify (Andreas, n.d.). The implied message has to be inferred by the coachee and it cannot be detected or found in the statement, as is the case with presuppositions. For example, the verb 'try' indirectly signals difficulty. Saying, *'Well, let's try to solve this'* implies a bit of a struggle which you may or may not want to convey, depending on context. On the other hand, remarking, *'You expected some difficulty. What did you notice about that this week?'* presupposes something happening and the word 'difficulty' is in the sentence. The message is less camouflaged than in the case of an implication. Let's examine another example:

   'When you experiment your new solution, please notice what happens so we can have plenty to discuss in our next session.'

This is a presupposition. It presupposes that something, possibly plenty, will happen.

| '*Not all changes happen during the session.*'

This is an implication. It can be inferred that change can take place outside the session (although using the word 'all' in 'not all changes' also presupposes that there will be changes during the session).

Implications and presuppositions need to be used skilfully and in a planned manner. Just as with seeding, you need to know specifically why you have decided to use it. What is the particular outcome you want to achieve? What responses do you aim to facilitate? When employed with a clear goal in mind, they can enhance motivation, receptivity and positive expectancy.

Manoeuvrability: keeping options open

Strategic coaches are clear about responsibilities. Coachees choose the presenting problem, decide on the desired goals and are responsible for doing the work required to accomplish them (Fisch et al. 1982). Strategic coaches are responsible for the process that will help coachees succeed and thus hold themselves accountable for any lack of results. Relinquishing responsibility for the coaching process would be doing a disservice to the coachee. Strategic coaches control the pacing and direction of the coaching session for a reason. They believe that coachees do not know how best to approach their goals and resolve their problems. If they did, they would not have consulted a coach in the first place (Fisch et al. 1982). This puts the responsibility on the strategic coach and the concept of manoeuvrability helps in that direction. This is no different to a coach who refuses to take on a corporate project because imposed restrictions will compromise the outcome. Manoeuvrability and restrictions cannot co-exist.

Maintaining manoeuvrability means keeping options open. It enables the coach to have the freedom to change actions and shift according to need as coaching progresses, with the intention of maximizing the contributions made to change (Fisch et al. 1982, Hart and Randell 2006). For example, when one position is no longer working, the coach is flexible enough to switch to another position (Quick 2012) and move in another direction. When a reframing does not seem to be working or when a task does not seem to sit well with the coachee, the coach can recall and redirect. The 'go slow' message previously described serves as a manoeuvring tactic as it offers the coach some wiggle room (Quick 2008, Quick 2012, Rohrbaugh and Shoham 2015, Rohrbaugh 2018). For manoeuvrability to be preserved, strategic coaches avoid conditions that will close off options and reduce freedom (Fisch et al. 1982). How do they keep their options open?

They keep their options open by not taking firm positions so that they are not constrained later (Hart and Randell 2006). If the direction they are following does not look promising, they can pull back from a particular stance or strategy rather than do more of what's not working (Fisch et al. 1982, Hart and Randell 2006, Quick 2008). Taking a definite position that does not sit well with the coachee can undermine credibility and rapport. Manoeuvrability allows you, as a strategic coach, to continually assess, adapt and suggest. Language, what I like to call 'manoeuvrability phrasing', also keeps options open. Using tentative words (Vaughn 2004) such as 'appear', 'seem' and 'maybe' does not denote a fixed reality and allows room to manoeuvre if what once appeared to be one way is now another.

One-down position

Showing one's expertise can inspire confidence but in may also intimidate or aggravate. Strategic coaches carefully balance an expert/non-expert stance. Using a one-down position such as *'Will you help me understand that a little more?'*, *'I wonder if you could give me some more information?'*, *'May I give a suggestion?'* encourages coachees to give more information and promotes co-operation. Power struggles are avoided and options are kept open if a shift in direction is needed.

This does not mean that suggestions are never given directly. Strategic coaches do not shy away from offering specific tasks and suggestions but it is done in a subtle, non-confrontational way. Rather than saying *'Here's what to do if you want to handle conflicts more effectively'*, the preferred option would be *'I am not sure how much this will benefit you* (implying that it will) *but if you could try to ...'* before proceeding with the suggestion.

If it is assessed as beneficial to the coachee, an 'expert' explanation may be provided. For instance, if the coachee doesn't understand why the same ineffective solution has been applied for so long (*'I just don't understand why I kept going on and on for so long when I could see that things were getting worse'*), the coachee will offer an answer that will normalize what the coachee was doing and minimize any self-blaming. Normalizing coachee responses is a very strategic thing to do:

Coach: *It's what most of us do. We're creatures of habit and habits are quite powerful. They keep us doing what we have always done. This partly explains the difficulty experienced in changing lifestyle habits such as eating and exercise. And most of us have not learned to move away from doing what's logical to what works even if it appears illogical ... Does it make sense now?*

Despite the preoccupation with directing the coaching process, strategic coaches are careful not to overtly exercise control but gently steer the coachee in a direction that will eventually break the pattern of problem-reinforcing solutions.

Behavioural assignments

Seeds are planted during coaching conversations but most change is expected to take place outside the session (Israelstam 1988). Therefore, homework assignments and experiments take up such a prominent position in the brief strategic model that they are considered to be the equivalent of what interpretation is to the traditional approaches: a basic tool of the process (Madanes 1991). Regardless of whether tasks are assigned in a straightforward manner or paradoxically, they are designed with common objectives in mind (Haley 1976, O'Hanlon 2000, Haley and Richeport-Haley 2003, Zeig 2006b, Quick 2008, Russel 2017, Yapko 2019). These are:

- To disrupt the coachee's problem-maintaining behavioural pattern. This can be achieved in a number of ways, such as introducing changes to the sequence, interactions, frequency, setting, performance and time of events.
- To encourage a new pattern or get the coachee to behave differently.
- To direct attention to a specific behaviour and the responses it generates.
- To test the accuracy of the coachee's perceptions and facilitate a new frame of mind.
- To gather information about the coachee's commitment to and readiness for change from their reactions and assignment delivery.
- To assess whether the coachee is moving in the right direction.
- To explore obstacles to goal attainment.
- To better integrate new learnings that arise during the session.
- To amplify thoughts and behaviours that will disrupt maladaptive patterns.
- To develop a realization of the coachee's contribution to problem formation and its solution.

Behavioural assignments are essentially practical interventions to move the coachee towards the desired goal. Because of their importance, it is advisable to start small and be specific about the actions that need to be taken or avoided to ensure that the coachee fully comprehends them. The assignments need to be carefully designed and tailored to the situation, as well as to the coachee's personality, style of communication and thinking (Craigie 1985). If, for example, the coachee is a researcher, the assignment could be a research experiment, and if the client is a writer, a narrative account of the findings may be suggested. By proposing a course of action (or no action), coachees become actively involved in the change process and come to their own conclusions via an experiential channel rather than an intellectual or informational one. Finally, all directives are purposeful, and the coach needs to have a learning goal in mind for the specific coachee in the specific situation.

Brief strategic coaching incorporates the steps of the original MRI process. These include understanding the complaint, clarifying the goal, identifying the attempted solution pattern that maintains or complicates the problem, and breaking the vicious cycle of problem maintenance by changing to more effective solutions that stem from a different perspective. To make it easier to understand and follow, the process has been broken down to three stages:

1 The clarification phase, during which the problem is defined, the desired goal is clarified and the first minimal steps are set.
2 The exploration phase, where attempted solutions are investigated and assessed.
3 The action phase, where the new designed strategy is introduced and the coachee starts to implement it to create the actual change.

But first things first. What's the problem?

4 The Clarification Stage: Define, Clarify, Set!

The change process starts the moment you greet the coachee. The first course of action centres on gathering data about the nature of the complaint. Brief strategic coaches take coachees' presenting complaint at face value and don't see it as the tip of an iceberg. The idea that a deeper exploration is required to really understand the problem implies that the client's difficulty is complicated and its handling requires an equally complex procedure. The pattern that emerges with this kind of handling, which a strategic coach wants to avoid, is similar to this:

- The coachee consults the coach and expresses concern about a problem that needs to be resolved. Individual efforts to cope with the complaint in the past have not been successful.
- The coach listens to the complaint and shares the perception that deeper digging is required. The coachee comes to expect an elaborate journey.
- The coachee embarks on an inner journey and explores deep-seated causes. If the problem doesn't resolve, it is an indication that the root cause is yet to be discovered. The desired change becomes conditional. Unless you uncover the underlying causes of the problem, resolution will not occur.
- As further insight is encouraged, coach and coachee further depart from the original complaint. Goal relevancy is reduced.

When addressing what the client brings to the table, you work with what they are motivated and ready to tackle (Weakland et al. 1974). Goals aren't redirected elsewhere, with the assumption that the coach knows better. Neither are assumptions being made on behalf of and for the client. Sessions only become relevant when their complaints are the object of coaching and this relevance creates a positive working alliance (Watzlawick et al. 1974/2011, Rohrbaugh and Shoham 2001, Quick 2008, Schöttke et al. 2014). Relevance stems from acknowledging what coachees perceive as their most important issues, respecting what is most pressing for them in the present and strengthening goal congruence.

Questions in strategic coaching are both a means of accumulating information and a means of influence. They gently steer the dialogue in a particular direction and keep the conversation focused (Healing and Bavelas 2011). The direction of the initial line of inquiry includes a two-fold objective: to define the problem and to clarify and set goals. In order to change, the coachee needs to act differently. In order to get them to *act* differently, the coach depends on a clear picture of how the coachee has been acting in the first place. This also pertains to other people who are associated with the client and the presenting complaint. That's why strategic coaches will invest a lot of time and effort in this step and are less hasty than their solution-focused counterparts to move to the 'do something different' stage of the conversation (Fisch et al. 1982, Eubanks 2002, Quick 2012). The information gathered in the problem investigation phase impacts success and any time spent in this stage is considered time very well spent (Fisch et al. 1982).

Before proceeding to the inquiry specifics, it should be noted that problem clarification focuses on client *complaints* and not on what the coach identifies as in need of change. The presence of a specific behaviour does not necessarily make it a problem, at least not for everyone (Quick 2008). A manager's lack of empathy, for example, may have an impact on interpersonal relationships both at work and in their personal life but it won't be a target for change unless the manager complains about it. The coach may consider it an area that requires improvement but, unless the manager brings it up as a problem, it won't be treated as one. If the same manager brings up a desire to change careers and pursue a dream that has long been kept at bay, that would become the focus of attention. This is evident in the strategic saying: 'If there is no complaint, there is no problem' (Fisch et al. 1982, Fisch and Schangler 1999, Quick 2008). In general, it's about meeting the client where the client is.

Defining the problem: What does it look like?

The strategic coach seeks to clarify the problem in concrete and action-orientated terms (Murphy and Duncan 2007). What prompted the client to seek coaching? What specifically are they hoping to change with your assistance that individual efforts have failed to achieve? You may be thinking that eliciting a behavioural depiction of the complaint is not unique to strategic work and so you may remain unimpressed with this line of inquiry. You have a point. It no longer is unique. However, when the MRI group favoured a shift of focus towards observable behaviour more than half a century ago, it ran counter to what was mainstream at that time. Their proposed focus of inquiry was unconventional and heavily criticized.

The initial conversation is guided by a question that is considered a hallmark of the brief strategic model (Fisch et al. 1982: 70):

'*Who* is doing *what* that presents a problem, to *whom*, and *how* does such behaviour constitute a problem?'

This is a mouthful of a question and not one you'll ask your coachee in one go. Coachees may have already reached the point of exhaustion as a result of their repetitive yet fruitless attempts to solve their problem. A strategic coach is careful to break the process into bite-sized pieces and make it as uncomplicated as possible so that the client can follow along. In keeping with the same mindset, let's simplify the question into three components and explore each one in further detail. You may also want to refer to the table at the end of the chapter, which includes a list of strategic detailing questions used to elicit behavioural information and to facilitate problem resolution.

Who is doing what that presents a problem?

When coachees are prompted to discuss what is troubling them, they often provide abstract definitions. 'I want to be happier', 'I want to feel more confident', 'My life's a mess', 'I have to up my game if I want to keep my job' are just a few typically vague statements. The task for the coach is to move from an abstract definition of the problem to a behavioural account of the situation by asking for specific examples that illustrate the complaint (Armatas 2019). A number of coachees may struggle to answer 'What made you pick up the phone and meet with me today?' because they are thinking in terms of causation or trying to detect underlying factors related to their problem (Quick 2008). In short, they are asking themselves the wrong question: 'Why am I having this problem?' or 'What's causing me this problem?', which is another way of asking 'Why?'. In all fairness, they have probably asked themselves Why?' many times before – as have family, friends and co-workers – so they assume your line of inquiry follows a similar direction. Being persistent in your exploration of *their doing* and clearly explaining that you are seeking nothing more than a description will encourage more helpful responses.

Intent on obtaining a behavioural description of the problem, the coach asks for specific examples in order to understand *who is doing what*. The collected information on what coachees and other involved parties are doing serves several purposes. It facilitates a better assessment of the already-attempted solutions explored in the next stage (the doing). This in turn helps to break the problem-maintenance pattern (stop the doing) and replaces the ineffective solution (a new doing). It maintains focus and keeps coachees engaged in action talk. It also serves as a clear distinction between being and doing.

Strategic professionals never identified their clients as being or even having a problem. Instead, they acknowledged them as inherently resourceful individuals who are not aware of how they are actively contributing to their problem. The coach, driven by this kind of mindset, seeks answers to how their clients are *doing* the problem. 'How are they doing stress?' 'How are they doing conflict?' 'How are they doing bad leadership?' or 'How are they doing underperformance?'. A characteristic question would be to ask the coachee to teach you how to acquire the same problem.

'I am wondering ... This is somewhat unconventional and not what you'd expect to hear ... But if we swapped roles and I were here to learn from you rather than the other way round ... And I told you that I have never experienced what you've just described and I'd like to learn from you ... Can you please teach me to have the same problem as you? Where do I start?'

This question has quite a bit going on. It comes from a top-down position. Pre-empting is employed before the end question is asked; the coaching session is framed as a learning process with an implied message that reads 'If the coach can learn to have it, the coachee can equally unlearn to have it'.

In keeping with a top-down position, when complaints remain abstract or are not clarified, the strategic coach may express confusion or a lack of understanding and will request further details. It is not unlikely to purposely downplay one's expertise to ensure that the coachee will not feel inept or pressured but will keep on helping with the clarification. Furthermore, a visual depiction of the problem may be requested, such as asking what one would see in a short video that would help to visualize the problem situation (O'Hanlon and Weiner-Davis 1989/2003, Gill 1999, Rohrbaugh and Shoham 2001). The following is a brief statement from the coach asking for a visual depiction in a top-down position while indicating confusion:

> *Please bear with me, I'm still a bit confused, would you give me more details?*
>
> *I haven't quite clearly understood and I need your help. What would I see if I had a video of the situation?*

What happens when coachees present themselves with an array of problems? Coachees may find it difficult to narrow down their focus to one problem or to choose one complaint while leaving the rest behind, even though not all of them are top priority or equally pressing. Calling attention to the difficulty of tackling several problems simultaneously and how it can compromise progress tends to ease their hesitancy. However, they will still need some help with the selection process. Straightforward questioning is often sufficient:

> *Which is currently the most pressing problem?*
> *What is the biggest pain point right now?*
> *Which will bring the biggest relief once resolved?*

The coach asks the questions but the coachee makes the final decision. Consider the following example:

Coach: *What brings you in here today?*
Coachee: Well, things are not going that well for me lately.
Coach: *In what way?*
Coachee: My work has gone downhill, I am making increasingly silly mistakes. I've worked hard to get to where I am today and I just don't seem able to concentrate like I used to ... To be honest, I am starting to lose my confidence, and I am irritable most of the time, snapping at everyone ... And my relationship is in trouble ... That's more than enough, isn't it?
Coach: *It certainly is a handful. I was wondering, which one is the most pressing for you?*
Coachee: They all are.

Coach: *I am sure they are. I am not implying that some aren't bothering you, they all are. The reason I am asking which one is bothering you the most, is that if we attempt to resolve all these difficulties concurrently, I am concerned that it will diffuse our focus and end up compromising our success, not unlike what you've probably been doing.*

Coachee: I see.

Coach: *Would that be OK?*

Coachee: I guess.

Coach: *We can always work on the rest if it's still needed but don't be surprised to see that, after resolving one problem, further changes continue in a ripple effect.*

Coachee: That's good, knowing we can still focus on the other issues as well.

Coach: *Of course we can.*

Coachee: OK, then ...

Coach: *Of all the problems you've mentioned, which one will bring the biggest relief when resolved?*

Coachee: My relationship ...

Coach: *So, that would offer the biggest relief? That's where the biggest gain will be?*

Coachee: Oh, yes, knowing that we're in a good place again.

Coach: *What exactly is the problem with the relationship?*

Coachee: I feel as if we are growing apart ...

Coach: *Growing apart?*

Coachee: Yes, becoming distant.

Coach: *How long have you been sensing a growing distance between the two of you?*

Coachee: On and off, about a year.

Coach: *And what are the signs of the growing distance?*

Coachee: The signs?

Coach: *Yes, if I had a video of the two of you doing distance, what would I see on the video clip which would get me thinking, 'Oh yes, there's definitely a growing distance between these two?'*

The client proceeds to describe the problem in more visual terms: what is being done and not done, what is being said and not said that indicates distancing.

To whom and how does it constitute a problem?

Having amassed the details of 'Who does what?', the area of interest is now directed 'To whom?' and 'How is it a problem?'. For example, when a client complains about being stressed or worried, the coach seeks information about what happened that led the coachee to feel that way. Asking for a description of events that led to the problem will not only illuminate 'Who does what?' but also 'To whom?', further clarifying the problem. If the coachee describes the complaint as low confidence, a corresponding question would be:

> *'You're saying that you feel as if you lack confidence at work. I am wondering what has happened that led to a slump in your confidence levels?'*

Inquiring in what way the complaint is a problem is a pivotal part of the conversation. As the brief strategic model is an interactional approach, social context is important, so exploring how the complaint is a problem for other people as well– not just the coachee – is essential (Fisch 2004, Quick 2008, Gonzalez et al. 2011). Investigating 'To whom is this a problem and in what way?' clarifies customership (see below for a definition). It may be that the complaint isn't much of an issue to the coachee but to someone else. Similarly, the 'Why now?' question can provide useful information (Rohrbaugh and Shoham 2001) and it can take you in two directions. Coachees can mention that the problem pains them more than they can handle or that they have much to lose if the issue is not resolved. Alternatively, they may reveal that their current efforts are the result of external pressures. In the former case, you have a strong motivational basis to call upon to engage your client throughout the coaching process. In the latter instance, you'll need to reassess customership and determine whether you are going to bring in the real customer.

Customership refers to whether the coachees are visitors, customers or complainants (Berg 1989, Cade 2001, Quick 2008). Did they request your assistance because of their own concern or the concern of others? (Cade 2001). This is not labelling your clients but ascertaining the type of working relationship you will have with them. If the client is a customer, they have contacted you on their own accord and are most likely to be motivated for change (Cade 2001). Using the words of Rohrbaugh and Shoham (2001: 9), 'they're the sweaters' and it's the sweaters who are most invested in the coaching process. They are ready to do the work, willing to carry out homework assignments and are generally committed to creating the desired change.

'Complainants' are also discomforted by the situation. They are keen to describe the problem and how it is impacting them but they're not so willing to do something about it. They're unaware of how they contribute to the problem or how they can contribute to its solution. The coach may want to delay assigning tasks until they are more actively involved in the process. Inquiring how things will be different when the problem is resolved, highlighting the soon-to-be changes and showcasing how their behaviour can improve the situation is likely to help complainants grow into customers.

Finally, 'visitors' are usually attending the session at someone else's request or insistence. They are not troubled by the problem and are definitely not sweating it out. They may be an employee who reluctantly follows a manager's request to attend but doesn't share the same perspective of the situation, a child who doesn't understand what the fuss is all about, even though their parents are at the end of their tether, or a business partner who believes that the associate is overreacting. In the case of visitors, the conversation often ends with a joint decision not to proceed with further sessions, although strategic coaches may try using paradox strategies before the decision is made (Cade 2001, Rohrbaugh 2018).

Clarifying and setting goals

Goals serve several key functions. They improve performance for both individuals and teams. They direct, motivate and energize. They fuel persistence and action (Locke and Latham 2002, Locke and Latham 2006), especially when they are not the result of external pressure, as in the case of a visitor, but are aligned with one's developing interests and values (Sheldon and Elliot 1999, Armatas 2015). Furthermore, an agreement between coach and coachee on goals as well as the nature of the complaint reduces the emotional impact of the presenting problem (Dormaar et al. 1989, Graham 2003). The prospects for goal success improve when the following criteria are met (Berg and Miller 1992, Coats et al. 1996, Locke and Latham 2002, Locke and Latham 2006):

- Goals are described in concrete, behavioural terms.
- Goals are shared rather than kept private.
- Goals are personally meaningful and important to the coachee. As a result, commitment is raised.
- Goals are challenging, realistic and attainable. They are difficult enough not to be tedious and small enough to create a positive expectancy of success.
- Goals are stated as the presence of a desired accomplishment, not the absence of an unwanted outcome.
- Goals are phrased as the beginning rather the end of something.
- Goal attainment efforts are accompanied by regular feedback and support.

By defining client goals in concrete terms and making them accomplishable (Watzlawick et al. 1974/2011), the coach sets the stage for applying effective solutions later in the process without getting caught up in another problem-maintaining cycle. Straightforward questioning will clarify the desired change: What would coachees like to be doing that their problem is blocking? How do they want things to change? How would their life or work be different when the problem is solved? If they are not experiencing the problem anymore, what would they be doing instead? If you, the coach, had a video of the resolved problem, what would you see?

When the desired change has been detailed, the coachee is encouraged to commit to a small workable goal. Asking what small amount of change is needed to acknowledge that the situation is improving allows for small-scale, non-threatening goals to be set (Rohrbaugh 2018). There are many variations that might work but the distinctive original strategic question is: '*What would be a first small sign that would tell you that you are moving in the right direction?*'. Two words stand out: 'small sign'.

Starting small is a common aspect of the strategic model and an integral part of its philosophy (Watzlawick 1974/2011, Fisch et al. 1982, Rohrbaugh and Shoham 2001, Fisch 2004, Quick 2008). When minimal goals are specified, their presence indicates that change has begun and they can be used to evaluate whether progress has been made and in what way (Watzlawick et al. 1974/2011, Fisch and Schangler 1999, Rohrbaugh and Shoham. 2001, Quick 2008, Carratala et al. 2016). At this point in the conversation, we mustn't be carried away and confuse what we hope to achieve with how we'll go about achieving it. It is strongly recommended that you keep the focus on the end result. The means to get there will be focused on at a later stage.

Coach: *What would be a first sign that would indicate things are taking a turn for the better and your efforts are starting to work?*

Coachee: Well, if I can say 'no' to a colleague's request without feeling guilty afterwards that would be a positive sign.

Coach: *When you feel guilty afterwards, what do you do? How do you handle that?*

Coachee: Well, I try to compensate by helping in other areas. I apologize more than I should. I bend over backwards to please in other ways, which ends up being more work than just saying 'yes' to what was requested in first place.

Coach: *I see … So a good first sign is to say 'no', which you have done before, but not compensate by bending over backwards and helping out in other ways due to the guilt, not apologizing other than perhaps for the initial 'I'm sorry but I can't help you this time round' type of response … Would that be correct?* (Turning feelings into behaviour.)

Coachee: Yes, that would be right.

Coach: *And what will you be doing instead?* (Focusing on the doing part of not feeling guilty and then proceeding to set the first small goals.).

In short, the change process starts the moment the coach strikes up a conversation with the coachee (Watzlawick et al. 1974/2011). The objectives to be met during this stage are as follows:

1 Keep the strategic dialogue current, focused and relevant.
2 Define the problem. Gather behaviourally described information that answers the question 'Who does what to whom and how does that behaviour constitute a problem?'.
3 Clarify the desired change; what does the client want to accomplish?
4 Inquire what small changes will indicate that the situation is taking a turn for the better and set them as the coachee's first minimal goals.
5 Recognize and utilize the language the coachee is using while talking about the problem and the desired change.
6 Plant the first reframing seeds to facilitate new behaviours in the final stage of the process.

Despite the objective of focused conversations, the strategic coach is responsible for creating a relationship where clients feel respected, understood, validated and acknowledged (Gonzalez et al. 2011, Ray and Schangler 2012). A word of caution is not to jump to solutions too soon before achieving problem and goal clarity. When this stage is successfully completed, the next task is to proceed to the exploration stage, where attempted solutions are investigated and assessed. Table 4.1 provides details of the strategic detailing process.

Table 4.1 Strategic detailing questions to elicit behaviourally described information

Strategic detailing questions:

CLARIFYING THE PROBLEM: *Who is doing what to whom and how does that constitute a problem?*
What can I help you with?
What exactly is the problem that brings you in today?'
What made you pick up the telephone to call me?'
Tell me a little bit more about what is going on.
If we had a short video of this, what would I see and hear?'
What do you do because of your problem that you want to stop doing or change?
What's the problem that brought you here today?
Can you describe a recent example?
What happens first? Then what happens? Then what?
Who is usually around when this happens?
How often does it happen?
How long does it last?
In what way is it a problem?
Is anyone else bothered by what is happening?
Why now?

PRIORITIZING PROBLEMS
Which problem is bothering you the most?
Which is the highest priority?
To make the most difference, where should we start?
Which is the most pressing problem for you?
Which problem is causing the most distress?
Which will bring the biggest relief once resolved?
Where is the biggest pain?

IDENTIFYING THE CLIENT
Who has the problem?
Whose decision was it to come here today?
Who else thinks that this is a problem?
Who is suffering the most?
Who is looking for help?
Who agrees with the need for coaching? Who does not?

Strategic detailing questions:

GOAL SETTING: *What would be a first small sign that would tell you that you are moving in the right direction?*
How do you want things to change?
What will happen or not happen that denotes change has started?
What would be the smallest change that you would be satisfied with?
How would your life/work be different when the problem is solved?
How would others notice that the problem is resolved? What would they do differently?
What would you be doing differently that would let you know that the situation is improving?
What behavioural changes, however small, would show that progress has been made?
What would indicate that you were on the right path?
How will you (or specific others) know that the situation is improving?
If I had a video of the problem resolved, what would I see?
If you are not experiencing the problem anymore, what would you be doing instead?
What would you like to be doing that your problem is blocking?

A signature question of the brief strategic approach.

5 The Exploration Stage: Explore and Assess Attempted Solutions

Since the problem is maintained and complicated by the very efforts the coachee and other parties involved are applying to the problem, it is essential to get a detailed account of what those efforts are (Fisch et al. 1982). This stage explores what solutions have been attempted in order to solve the problem and achieve the goals. Exploring the coachee's attempted solutions is the most critical part of the strategic coaching process and what sets it apart from other models. Solution-focused professionals, for instance, are not likely to invest time assessing ineffective solution tactics. Even when they do, they are swifter to direct their intention towards amplifying what is already working (Quick 2012). Strategic coaches emphasize the importance of investigating and evaluating what is not working because that is how problems are inherently formed. The intervention proposed in the final stage that will lead to successful problem resolution and goal attainment is based on the information gathered in this step (Watzlawick et al. 1974/2011, Fisch and Schlanger 1999, Saggese and Foley 2000, Quick 2008, Pitt et al. 2015, Rohrbaugh and Shoham 2015).

Eliciting prior and current solution attempts involves the use of open questions which direct attention to the class of solutions already tried and tested by the coachee and other people. Although gathering information about ineffective strategy implementations (Hart and Randell 2006) may be relatively simple, there is a three-fold goal to be achieved during this step. The three objectives are to:

1 explore the attempted solutions that have been implemented by the coachee and others
2 examine the effectiveness of the attempted solutions
3 look for the common theme underlying the coachee's attempted solutions.

1. Explore attempted solutions by client and others

Directly inquiring what the client did to resolve the problem should suffice and provide the necessary information. Although prior solutions are also explored, the focus is on current ones (Fisch et al. 1982). Exploring how the coachee has been endeavouring to deal with the problem will reveal which of the three types of maladaptive solutions was applied. Is it that action was taken at the wrong level? Is it that action was not needed but the client acted in anticipation of a potential difficulty or was it that no action was taken when there should have been? Solution efforts and advice from other people in the coachee's life must also be scrutinized. What have others been trying to do in the hope of helping? The main interest is in investigating quicksand-type approaches to problem resolution, where the more you struggle to keep afloat the faster and deeper you sink.

There follows a sample of questions to elicit information about attempted solutions by the coachee or others involved in the situation that have been maintaining and reinforcing the problem.

What do you do when this happens?
How has your manager or partner (or any other person involved) tried to help?
What have you tried to do to solve this problem?
How have you tried to deal with this situation before coming here?
What have you tried in an attempt to prevent this from happening?
In what way have you tried to decrease or eliminate the problem?
What have you been doing to help yourself so far? What have others been doing?
Who has tried to help you? In what way?
Were you given any advice on how to tackle this problem?
What do you usually do in situations like these?
Have you tried anything else to reduce the problem?
Anything else?

Anything else? is a short yet powerful follow-up question and it cannot be stressed enough how valuable it can be in generating extra details. A little bit of extra prompting may uncover a lot more information on solution tactics which may have otherwise remained under the blanket. It is worth asking coachees whether there were any solutions they initially thought of implementing but eventually discarded as potentially unhelpful. Their answers may reveal that they did think of different solution tactics only to reject them soon after because they were just not logical enough for serious consideration (Heath and Atkinson 1989). In the occasional case that coachees reply that they have tried nothing at all, don't immediately take it at face value. The sense of inescapability which is inherent in every problem compels us to search for a way out. The instinctual response when trapped is to look for the exit and set ourselves free. It is rare for someone to pick up the phone and schedule an appointment with you without having unsuccessfully tried to handle the problem on their own, unless you're not dealing with the real customer but the visitor.

There is an additional explanation for why some coachees may say they have tried nothing even if that is not the case. They assume you are asking about implemented solutions that have been successful. One way to work through this is to mention a couple of solution choices other people make in similar situations and ask if they have tried any similar practices (Quick 2008). A question to a coachee who has been feeling self-conscious during meetings at work, for example, could be:

> 'When people are in a similar situation, they try to relax as a way to cope better. Another common practice is to use distraction. Some people try to avoid them altogether. Does that sound familiar? Were your first instincts to try something similar or did you go about it in a different way?'

Attentive listening to the client's description of solution efforts is key. Coachees may be describing attempts to deal with the emotions associated with the problem rather than trying to resolve the problem *per se* (Quick 2008). For example, a professional athlete with more than a few distinctions in his career has seen his performance lagging. When he states 'It's not getting better no matter what I do', he offers a perfect transition to an attempted solutions inquiry. When asked 'What have you done?', he mentions engaging in comforting thoughts and relaxation exercises so that anxiety won't take over. At first glance, these solution practices seem to be answering your question but if you ask 'When do you try to relax?', you may discover that it's after the event. This means that the tactics are a means of dealing with the emotional impact of an inadequate performance rather than with the performance directly. To clarify this further, you may want to ask about solution practices before and during his race in an effort to get back on the winning side.

2. Examine the effectiveness of attempted solutions

Once attempted solutions data have been gathered, their effectiveness or lack of it is carefully examined. Simply asking 'Was it helpful?', 'What happened when you (or someone else) did that?', 'How did that work out?' or 'What were the results?' is sufficient to get an idea of whether the attempted solution in question passes the test. Not all attempted solutions are guaranteed to be effective. Certain tactics may have been successful in the past but currently remain unexploited. Coachees may not have reapplied a solution that was once successful in dealing with a similar situation because they did not expect to experience it again.

There is the assumption that, if a problem reappears in the future, the solution was not truly effective and a search for a different one commences. It may be the case that, after a tiresome effort to solve a problem, some coachees will jump at the opportunity for much-needed relief and relaxation. As they enjoy the fruits of their labour, they may also ease their efforts and return to habitual and less effective behaviours. Or they simply forget that the solution to their problem is not a one-off occurrence and reapplication is necessary (O'Hanlon and Weiner-Davis

1989/2003). In either case, when prior effective actions have been identified, the once-tested solution in the past can be retested in the current setting.

Concerning their problem-reinforcing solutions, the objective is to help coachees evaluate their solution strategies and infer that they are actually adding to their problem rather than solving it. This will pave the way for accepting a new viewing and doing of the problem in the next stage. Strategic coaches prefer not to directly tell their clients to stop what they are doing. The rationale for avoiding 'don't commands' in an effort to steer coachees away from ineffective solution tactics is explicit. 'Don't commands' represent a problem-reinforcing solution. Telling someone what they should not do reinforces their commitment to prove you are wrong and are drawn to do more of what you have requested they stop doing. Paradox is at work here but it is not in the client's interest. It is recommended that coachees contemplate the helpfulness or lack of helpfulness of their solution efforts by answering open-ended questions rather than being confronted head-on about their choices.

In the following interaction, Michael has been having a difficult time dealing with a well-mannered colleague who manages to repeatedly second-guess his input during meetings. He has clarified the problem to the coach and has set the first minimal goals. He proceeds to describe his coping methods.

Coach: *And what do you do when that happens?*
Michael: What do I do?
Coach: *Yes, when we are faced with a difficulty, our first instinct is to do something to help ourselves.*
Michael: (Nods.)
Coach: *How do you try to handle the situation when it happens?*
Michael: I try to hide my stress – I won't give him the pleasure of knowing that he has any impact on me but mostly I avoid eye contact with him. I concentrate on others, hoping it will make me less of a target.
Coach: *Has that been working?*
Michael: No.
Coach: *No?*
Michael: No, not at all.
Coach: *Well, what you've been doing is logical ... But logic hasn't been making the cut, has it?* (Seeding the idea of an 'illogical' direction at a later stage.)
Michael: No.
Coach: *Over time, have things improved, remained stable or taken a turn for the worse?*
Michael: It's gotten out of hand ... He just won't stop...
Coach: *I see ... Am I correct to say that trying to remain calm and keeping a low profile to avoid undue attention has not only been unhelpful but has possibly escalated matters? Am I getting it right?* (One-down position and focusing on how the solution is making matters worse.)
Michael: Yes.
Coach: *Anything else you have tried?*

Caution needs to be exercised during this stage. It is important that evaluating attempted solutions do not come off as evaluating the coachee. If clients feel judged and graded, they will withhold information on their past and current solution choices; information that is critical in helping them. One way to ensure that coachees feel comfortable, while realizing that their solution tactics have not been working and are possibly exacerbating the problem they are trying to resolve, is to normalize their choices. Emphasizing that their strategies are guided by reason and common sense helps put them at ease, keeps self-esteem intact and gets them thinking about the problem-maintaining qualities of their attempts (Rohrbaugh 2014).

Contrary to popular belief, the problem is not that coachees have been acting irrationally but that they have been acting too logically for their own good (Fisch et al. 1982, Fisch and Schlanger 1999). After normalizing their attempted solutions as the logical way to go about problem-solving, we can introduce the idea that the logical way may in fact be the least appropriate way. But first we need to detect the common thread underlying their choice of solutions.

3. Look for the common theme underlying the attempted solutions

While exploring attempted solutions, coachees will relay various ways of dealing with their problem. It may seem that they are describing different solution tactics but there is usually a common theme that runs through all their efforts (Fisch et al. 1982). Upon closer inspection, the attempted solutions are not essentially different but are variations of the same theme, branches of the same tree. Consider the athlete who tries to solve his underperformance through breathing techniques, distraction or positive affirmations. All his actions are geared towards a similar objective: to relax. Think of parents who are dealing with a demanding and non-collaborative child. They will tell you that they have tried everything to no avail. They have politely and calmly asked the child to 'behave', they have taken away privileges, they have threatened, scolded, offered advice, pleaded, bribed and the list goes on. These may appear to be different strategies but they all convey the same message and are unified under one intent: 'You must obey'. With that in mind, all attempts are considered as one strategy rather than many. By applying solutions that stem from the same theme we create first-order change (Fisch et al. 1982) when it's second-order change that we most likely need.

First-order and second-order change

The MRI strategic model distinguishes between first-order and second-order change (Watzlawick et al. 1974/2011, Fisch et al. 1982, Fraser and Solovey 2007). Applying a set of solutions that are governed by the same theme leads to first-order change. Let's revisit Virginia Satir and her stubbornness case. If the parent's attempts to render their daughter more co-operative had been working, first-order change is all that will be required. Coaching the parents to have more productive conversations with their daughter, reinforcing consistency in their behaviour and offering variations to their current set of solutions to make them more effective are all examples of first-order change. Assumptions regarding stubbornness are not challenged in this case and all strategies are directed to seeing it toned down. Another example would be a tutor of a young student (Fisch and Schlanger 1999). The child is not particularly engaged in the lesson. If the tutor's prompts to get down to business seem to be working, the message 'You need to concentrate and do your work' may suffice.

If the attempted solutions are not working, applying variations of the same belief will continue not to work. It will prolong the problem and likely make it worse. In this case, second-order change is required, which involves challenging the assumptions that govern behaviour. Second-order change solutions are strikingly different from the strategies applied in first-order change and appear to move in the opposite direction. Whereas first-order change solutions are common-sensical, second-order tactics usually seem illogical, counterintuitive and paradoxical. It is second-order change that disrupts the system. Virginia Satir created second-order change by reframing stubbornness into an asset and an achievement (Grinder and Bandler 1982). The solution of reducing or squashing the behaviour is replaced by respecting or even reinforcing it. The tutor will create a second-order change when she decides to modify her thinking and prescribes breaks instead of trying to prevent disengagement. Rather than telling the student 'Will you please concentrate and stop looking out the window?', she may opt for 'Why don't you take a five-minute break? I know it's been a long day and you need to clear your mind', which to the tutor's surprise might reduce overall distraction during the lesson and improve engagement when the break is over.

The following example may further clarify first-order and second-order change. Imagine that you have finished writing a book and have just printed your manuscript for a final proofread. The pile of papers is on the kitchen table and you have opened the door to get some breeze to mitigate the summer heat. All of a sudden, a strong gust of wind sends the papers flying about in the air. You jump from your chair and start chasing the scattered papers, grabbing as many as you can and holding them tight so they don't end up flying out of the door. That's your solution attempt. You may come up with various ideas of being efficient at salvaging your manuscript and, if you're not alone at home, you may enlist help. An extra set of hands would come in useful. All these efforts are examples of first-order change. The underlying perception of the situation and the solution is to 'grab and save the papers'. A second-order change results from a different assumption. You don't try to salvage the papers. You avoid paper-chasing attempts altogether. Instead, you get up and shut the door.

It's important to note that, when first-order change is sufficient to bring the coachee to the desired goal, the coach is advised to put the client's strengths to good use, refine their skills, tweak their strategies to make them more effective or direct them on a variant path that shares the same thinking. To attempt second-order change when first-order interventions would be efficient would perpetuate the problem and make its resolution a much more complicated process. The coach falls prey to taking action at the wrong level.

Planning the 'intervention'

The strategic data gathered in this stage allows us to get to know the problem through its solutions (Nardone and Portelli 2005). Exploring and assessing attempted solutions provides us with the information needed to design the intervention that will break the vicious cycle of problem maintenance. It literally influences the direction the coaching process will take. When we identify the common theme of the attempted solutions, we are soon aware of what to avoid – what not to do that's just more of the same (Fisch et al. 1982). Knowing what solutions to avoid, however, is not the end of strategic coaching.

Breaking the pattern may initially stop the problem maintenance but, unless it is replaced with another solution tactic that follows a different theme, any benefits are likely to be short-lived and reminiscent of a pause rather than change (Quick 2008). A radically different theme is often necessary to reverse the after-effects of prior coping strategies. For example, if the ineffective attempted solution entailed making someone stop a certain behaviour, the new solution may be to invite it instead. If the ineffective attempted solution was to hide one's anxiety, the new direction may be to advertise it. If the ineffective attempted solution was telling, the new direction may be asking or vice versa. Such a dramatically different alternative handling requires a change in the coachee's perspective (Fisch et al. 1982), which is why an array of strategies is employed in that direction from the very first session. In the next final stage, these strategies are utilized even more than before so that the new strategy is successfully introduced and the coachee begins implementing it.

To briefly summarize before moving to the final step of the brief strategic process, the objectives to be met during this stage are as follows:

1 Explore attempted solutions implemented by the coachee and others. Although prior solutions will be covered, the focus is on current solution attempts.
2 Examine the effectiveness of attempted solutions. Help coachees come to their own conclusions and realize how their well-intended solutions are contributing to the problem.
3 Discern whether first-order change suffices or if second-order change is required.
4 Look for the common theme underlying the coachee's attempted solutions. This is where most of the reframing takes place, with the intent of altering the viewing of both problem and solutions, if second-order change is required. By changing the viewing, one can change the doing.

5 Identify the class of solutions that need to stop, the new strategies that will replace the old and the different theme that will govern them.

6 Keep on matching language and communications style to the coachee.

7 Keep on planting reframing seeds to facilitate acceptance and implementation of new solutions in the next stage.

6 The Action Stage: Introduce and Implement New Solution

The strategic process is a journey during which the coach *explores* (problem, goal and solution exploration), *prepares for change* (reframing, seeding and indirect suggestions) and finally *delivers* (introducing and implementing a new solution that creates change). The initial role of coach-explorer has come to an end and the focus is now on inducing the desired change. This is where we hand over the goods, so to speak, and put them to good use (Nardone and Salvini 2007). Coach and coachee collaborate to generate a new solution that goes beyond the 'do something different' advice. It is not just about doing something different but doing something different which stems from a different perspective and creates a second-order change – hence the importance of reframing.

There are various ways to disrupt an unsuccessful pattern (de Shazer 1985, O'Hanlon and Weiner-Davis 1989/2003, O'Hanlon 2000). These may be adding or removing an element from a problem, changing the frequency or sequence of behaviour, and changing the location, duration or time it occurs. The strategic coach, despite playing an active role in the coaching process, does not have a predetermined idea of how the coachee has attempted to solve the presenting problem and what will help them to exit the vicious cycle of problem maintenance. Each session remains a process of discovery and each individual plan is formulated based on the client's attempted solutions history. In the two previous stages, specific data have been gathered that will help to answer key questions. It is the answers to the following questions that will determine the type of intervention to be administered (Fisch et al. 1982).

What is the coachee's perception that needs changing? What's the common theme?
Which are the attempted solutions to be abandoned?
Which action is a clear departure for the coachee's attempted solution?
Which new perception will facilitate such a departure? What will the change to the theme be?
Which attempted solutions have been most central to the problem?
Does the suggested action mediate the most prominent problem-maintenance handling?

While the resolution of the problem requires coachees to depart from their previous attempts, we cannot simply tell them to stop doing something without suggesting an alternative in its place. The objective is to secure an agreement with coachees about doing something they have never done before. Strategic interventions are initiated to serve this objective.

Intervention: introducing the new solution strategy

The new suggested strategy should not be much of a shock for coachees since a change of direction has already been carefully implied, seeded and slightly reframed. In addition, doubts have been cast throughout the previous step on the (in)effectiveness of their attempts and their underlying beliefs. Finally, it has been insinuated more than once that acting logically can cause trouble. Still, the strategic coach continuously sets the stage to maximize client consensus and collaboration. After all, the whole plan from the start was to get to this action phase as smoothly as possible.

The term 'intervention' is used quite frequently in strategic circles and this is an appropriate time to explain what we mean by it. An intervention is not an imposition. It does not imply that a certain action is forced upon the coachee. It refers to suggesting a different behaviour or action with the objective of intervening and breaking the problem-maintenance cycle. Offering input, assigning homework, giving feedback, reflecting observations, highlighting strengths, amplifying desired responses, seeding, reframing and redirecting focus are but a few of what are considered interventions.

Setting the stage for the introduction of the new solution can look like the following brief interaction, which takes place with a micromanager who has been stifling team managers' contributions in an attempt to deliver agreed-upon goals.

Coach: *Looking at your efforts to improve the bottom line, it seems that they all involved an attempt to enhance control. And it makes sense – our instinctive response when something appears to be getting out of our hands is to try to gain more control over it, isn't it?* (The dialogue starts with a reminder of the theme underlying the manager's behaviours and normalizes those behaviours.)

Coachee: Yes.

Coach: *It does make sense to initially move in that direction, doesn't it?* (Using the word 'initially' implies that after a while it will no longer seem as sensible.)

Coachee: Yes ...

Coach: *And from what you have described, it caused a bit of a rift in your relationship with your team and their performance ... Am I getting this right?* (Matching the manager's own words and taking a one-down position.)

Coachee: Yes, that's about right. Things are not going well between us.
Coach: *In line with what we have discovered* (the word 'we' points to a co-journey) ... *Is it fair to say that we need to rethink and move in a different direction in order to get different results, rather than keep on doing more of the same?*
Coachee: I guess so ...
Coach: *So, what do you guess could be a move in a different direction?*

Although you have designed a specific solution strategy that fits the client and the presenting problem, it is recommended that you lead the coachee to the action rather than directly suggesting it. That way, the coachee will have reached that conclusion on their own and won't feel that it was imposed. Owning it will also improve their commitment to follow through. If the manager replies that they don't know what might be a move in a different direction, the coach can indicate that a different direction is likely to be an opposite direction and rephrase the question:

> 'What could be different to trying to increase control? What could you do that would be in a different direction than "I need to control them more"?'

If the coachee cannot think of a different solution, it may be that the reframing wasn't successful enough or that you didn't manage to cast enough doubt on the attempted solutions in the solution assessment phase. It may make good sense to invest more time in understanding the client's perspective and reframing it. When coachees are given specific strategy suggestions that are consistent with their understanding of the situation, they perceive the new solution as less risky and are more likely to implement it (Watzlawick et al. 1974/2011, Quick 2008). Some strategic coaches, however, introduce the new solution directly after reframing has taken place. In order to further facilitate an agreement on testing out the new proposed behaviour, pre-empting is used (Watzlawick et al. 1974/2011). Just a brief reminder: in pre-empting, we express what we anticipate may get in the way before the coachee expresses it.

> 'There is a solution I'd like to suggest. This may sound a bit risky and I hope this won't be too difficult for you or too early to give it a go but how about ...?'

The strategic coach may decide to introduce the new solution tactic in the form of a paradox and wait for the next session to clarify it. By telling a coachee who wants to effectively tackle procrastination *'Don't accomplish anything yet, at least not until our next session'* may lead to a rise in productivity (Wachtel and Wachtel 1986). The coachee tends to defy the coach's request not to change or to deliberately act out the problem and, in doing so, moves towards the desired goal. In the next session, the coachee realizes that what was achieved is indicative of having control over the problem and the solution. Furthermore, the coach can explain the idea behind the paradox and introduce both how the problem was maintained and the new, drastically different solution.

> *'This is a good time to explain why I asked you not to accomplish anything these two weeks. I know you were quite perplexed to hear such awkward advice but I wanted you to experience firsthand how taking the pressure off productivity can make you more productive instead. All your attempts to deal with your situation had one thing in common. You tried to force productivity in a variety of ways which made the problem worse. Your way out, as illogical as it initially seemed, is to cut yourself some slack. Does that resonate with your experience?'*

Implications and presuppositions are put to use throughout this stage at the coach's discretion. In the procrastination paradox just described, you can detect them twice. In both examples, the message conveyed is that a) accomplishment will come at a later time (*'Don't accomplish anything yet ...'*) and b) after the initial reaction, what was illogical will be reconsidered as quite logical (*'As illogical as it may initially seem ...'*).

More than in any other stage, coaches will use as many strategies as are deemed necessary to help the coachee attain the desired change. One of the biggest contributors to a greater prospect of success is to start small. Starting small makes the goal more manageable, more comfortable, less ominous and easier to implement, and allows time to process any changes that occur in between sessions. When a small but strategically planned step takes place, it is expected to trigger further change in a domino effect (Fisch and Schlanger 1999). That is why the paradoxical 'go slow' message is widely used in brief strategic coaching.

Follow-up sessions

The main objectives in the follow-up sessions are to:

1 monitor, reinforce and solidify positive behaviour
2 frame the interval among sessions as improvement periods
3 confirm that sessions are effective and are leading towards the goal
4 prevent or deal with obstacles to goal attainment
5 link the new solutions strategy to the desired changes and further distance them from previous ineffective tactics
6 tweak interventions as needed or make a U-turn if the new strategy doesn't move the coachee close to the goal
7 sustain a new more effective problem-solving mindset
8 verify that the presenting problem is successfully resolved and that there is no other complaint in need of handling (de Shazer 1994).

In the following sessions, the coachee is invited to share information about the homework assignments and the new solution strategy. Questions such as *'What has happened since our last session?'* or *'What is different since the last time we met?'* are popularly used by the coach. Not only do they generate important information but they also imply that something has happened and that something is different. This is likely to trigger an inner search to detect signs of positive change (Gonzalez et al. 2011, Quick 2008). However, if the time between sessions has not been fruitful, these questions are not the most appropriate. On a personal note, if I cannot infer good news from the coachee's demeanour compared to the previous session, I favour the following more neutral question: *'What have you noticed these couple of weeks?'* Alternatively, the inquiry can start with the coach's first fail-safe observations:

Coach: *I detect a change in your mood since last time we met, am I right?*
Coachee: Yes, you are!
Coach: *So, there have been changes?*
Coachee: Yes!
Coach: *Tell me all about it …*

When the coachee describes positive change, the coach may, in addition to highlighting the new solution's effectiveness, suggest slow progress and caution against fast improvements. This is particularly the case with coachees who may appear overly optimistic or anxious, or where drastic change has occurred in a short period of time. Asking coachees to take all the time they need or even asking them to slow down to better solidify their successes helps to reduce the pressure of change by not making it a race and prevent disappointment from a possible setback. Depending on context and coachee, the coach may go as far as to ask for a planned 'relapse' some time the following week. Planning a relapse not only prevents a possible let down but it also increases control over the behaviour. The moment you plan something is the moment you exercise more control over it.

One way to encourage 'going slow' is when the coachee complains that the problem is still present and not entirely gone. If a coachee who has been procrastinating mentions that, despite some improvement, there are still delays in doing the required work, the coach may positively reframe it and use paradox by asking the client to hold on to a bit of that procrastination for a little while (Quick 2008, Gonzalez et al. 2011).

In strategic coaching, sessions are scheduled flexibly, in accordance with the needs of the coachee and the situation. Coach and coachee don't predetermine how often they will meet and there are no regular fixed meetings. Six sessions, for example, can be utilized in three months for one client and the same number of meetings will be spaced over seven months for another client. Intervals between sessions are shorter at the beginning of the coaching process and, as changes start to appear, longer intervals are established. It may be the case that coach and coachee decide, after spacing the sessions out at longer intervals, to reinstate more frequent meetings and then change back again.

If the coachee expresses the desire to work on another problem when the presenting complaint is resolved, a break is recommended before resuming a second round (Fisch et al. 1982). The client needs some time to consolidate their learning and to process the changes that resulted from the previous sessions. On a personal note, I may schedule an appointment with a longer interval than usual and give them a task. I will suggest that the coachee goes through the same process and comes back with an account of attempted solutions and their underlying common theme. I will hold back from asking them to come up with a new strategy, although it is often the case that the client returns having experimented in new ways.

As the problem is being resolved and the coaching journey comes to an end, it is recommended that coachees are prepared for meeting future challenges and crises. What are the anticipated hurdles? How will they deal with them without reverting to former solution attempts? Are the steps of defining the problem and goal, reviewing ineffective attempted solutions and disrupting the problem-maintenance cycle clear enough to be internalized by the coachee? Can the coachee go through the same process independently without the need for a coach? Learning how to independently identify the vicious cycle of faulty solution attempts and break the pattern promotes greater autonomy and it should not be overlooked (Soo-Hoo 1997, Armatas 2010).

Terminating the coaching process

The coaching process is terminated when there is no complaint. This is in line with the strategic motto 'If there's no complaint, there's no problem' (Fisch and Schlanger 1999). Because brief strategic work is, by definition, not a long process, termination is not that much of a big deal (Fisch et al. 1982). It's an event without fireworks. An additional reason that termination does not stand out is the strategic belief that change is possible and that the client has the inner resources to make it happen. So, when it does happen, it seems perfectly logical.

It is often the case that clients express their satisfaction with the outcome by accrediting the coach with the successful results. A strategic coach doesn't accept this accolade – although it may feel good – because to do so would disqualify the accomplishments and hard work of the coachee. Praising the coach can be seen as an opportunity to refocus on the coachee and highlight their contributions to success by helping the coach with problem clarification and setting the first meaningful goals, focusing on the present despite the temptation to analyse the past, displaying a willingness to experiment with a new solution despite it being contrary to the previous one and co-operating with the coach throughout the process.

When success does not come

When strategic suggestions do not bring about the desired change, or when coachees attend sessions without following through their homework assignments – either because they forgot, had no time or started having doubts about their validity – the coach assumes full responsibility and will look into possible causes. Table 6.1 can be used as a checklist or a brief guide for when your strategy fails, in order to detect what may need to be revisited and modified (Watzlawick et al. 1974/2011, Fisch et al. 1982, Quick 2008). This is where manoeuvrability comes in handy.

Table 6.1 A guide to identifying and managing obstacles to strategic success

Is the coachee the real customer?	Reassess customership. Even if the coachee was a customer, customership may have changed during the process. If the client is a complainant, can they become a customer? Would it be a good idea to bring in someone else to the session?
Are you working on the problem that is causing the biggest pain to the coachee?	If there is more than one complaint, you may want to reprioritize and ensure that you are working with the problem that is most discomforting for the client.
Is the complaint clear and behaviourally described?	Elicit clear, behavioural information about the complaint.
Is the goal unrealistic or no longer appropriate?	Revisit the problem clarification stage, retrace your steps and revise the original goal as needed.
Was the wrong strategy chosen and implemented?	Review the intervention and the thinking behind it. Re-examine the attempted solutions. Did you base your intervention on the faulty solution pattern? Did you get the coachee's common underlying theme correct? If so, was your suggested strategy in a different, if not opposite, direction than the coachee's?
Was second-order change necessary?	Reassess attempted solutions and their results. Would first-order change have been perfectly adequate?
Was the new solution strategy presented to align with the coachee's position?	Retrace your reframing efforts, detect any flaws and keep on reframing until the coachee understands.
Did you match the coachee's language and communication style?	Use the coachee's language and communicate in a way that is familiar to them.

Did you jump to new solutions too soon?	Revisit the problem clarification and the ineffective attempted solutions stages. Spend as much time as needed to gather all the information in order to design the most helpful intervention for the coachee and the situation. Moreover, this will allow the coachee more time to link their handling efforts to problem maintenance, and facilitate the uptake of a different direction.
Did the coachee understand the steps involved in the assigned task?	Ensure that the offered suggestions are clear, concise and positively stated. The coachee needs to understand precisely what to do and how to do it.
Was the assigned task a big step for the coachee? Was there too much inconvenience involved?	Start and proceed small so that it will feel less risky and intimidating. Assess whether the assigned steps are easily integrated in the coachee's daily life.
Did intervention involve action or was it limited to words?	Action creates change. Use words to encourage and support action.
Did you approach the client from a one-up position?	Prefer a one-down position that enhances collaboration, and reduces power struggles and confrontation. One-up positions may be employed, for example, when the client has been unco-operative and after careful consideration. It is not how we start.

7 Putting it into Practice

We appreciate theories _and research that inform our_ coaching practice. As practitioners, we also value the importance of knowing how to apply the theoretical frameworks in practice. This chapter aims to make strategic theory relevant. It illustrates several examples of strategic conversations that will help improve your understanding of the process and how to implement it successfully. Table 7.1 provides an overview of the brief strategic coaching framework that has been covered in previous chapters. It can serve as a reminder of the process when conducting your first brief strategic sessions with clients or employees.

Table 7.1   The brief strategic process at a glance

BRIEF STRATEGIC COACHING

The clarification stage: define, clarify, set!
   Objectives:
- Define the presenting complaint:
  'Who does what to whom and how does that behaviour constitute a problem?'
- Prioritize problems
- Clarify the desired change
- Set first minimal goals
  'What would be a first small sign that would tell you that you are moving in the right direction?'
- Assess customership: Who is the client?

The exploration stage: explore and assess attempted solutions
   Objectives:
- Explore attempted solutions by the client
- Explore attempted solutions by others
- Examine the effectiveness of all attempted solutions
- Look for unifying theme
- Discern whether first-order or second-order change is required
- Plan intervention: what perception needs to change, what solutions need to stop and what will replace them, what direction needs to be taken

---

BRIEF STRATEGIC COACHING

The action stage: introduce and implement new solution
  Objectives:
  - o Use strategies to alter coachee's viewing and doing of the situation (strategies most likely to succeed have gently started in previous stages and are now being maximized)
  - o Introduce new solution strategy
  - o Assign tasks to move in suggested direction
  - o Support implementation of new solution
  - o Refine and adapt as needed
  - o Terminate when goal achieved

The more I comfort her, the poorer her performance

Michelle is a mother of four. Her three older children are all health professionals who live in different cities. Her youngest daughter, Jenny, will be sitting for her university exams in less than two months.

Coach: *What can I help you with?*
Michelle: I am concerned about my daughter, Jenny. It's her turn for the university exams in June.
Coach: *Her turn?*
Michelle: Yes, I have three older children, all of whom have finished their studies and are now health professionals.
Coach: *So, that's some additional pressure for her.*
Michelle: Indeed, and this year's events haven't helped.
Coach: *What do you mean?*
Michelle: There were unexpected curriculum changes which stressed out both teachers and children … and her aunt, whom she adores, had a heart attack. She looks up to her and to see her look so fragile was very difficult to deal with. (Michelle is expressing the reason *why* she believes her daughter is dealing with the problem she will soon describe. Although she is talking about the past and possible causes, she needs to be heard and acknowledged. It also provides information about the context of her concerns. She will be directed to the here and now at a later time.)
Coach: *I see.*
Michelle: Thankfully, she is recovering well, so that's going OK now. And then the pandemic. Strangely enough, Jenny started to relax following the decision to close schools. I think it comforted her to know that she could put in more hours studying at home and better prepare for the exams.

Coach: *What seems strange in the beginning can make sense later. And it does make sense in a way, doesn't it?* (Seeding a possible illogical solution, normalizing behaviour and maintaining manoeuvrability just in case she gives information that may have a different interpretation.)

Michelle: Yes, she organized her time better and she scored very high in her mock exams.

Coach: *Scored? Past tense? Has that changed now?* (Directing her to the present.)

Michelle: Yes, it changed after she talked to a couple of her classmates and felt that she was falling behind in comparison ... and it got worse when the TV announced that schools were going to resume on 11 May. She has become very stressed and is not accepting any kind of help, such as seeing a professional or do something that will relax her. (The message 'You need to relax' is evident in her suggestion and gives a first clue that efforts to relax Jenny may not be the way to go.)

Coach: *I see, and what does Jenny's stress look like?* (Getting a clearer behavioural description of stress.).

Michelle: She is having these outbursts. It usually starts late evening. She doubts herself, claims she's not ready and needs more time to prepare ... and then sobs about being almost certain of her upcoming failure.

Coach: *You're present when that happens?*

Michelle: Yes, I'm right there.

Coach: *Is anyone else present when she has those self-doubt instances?* (Reframing outbursts as self-doubt instances.)

Michelle: No, just me.

Coach: *What do you do when that happens? How do you handle it?*

Michelle: I'm glad she chooses me to be the shoulder to cry on. I sit right next to her and I hold her in my arms. I try to comfort her and remind her that she needs to have more trust in her abilities. (Michelle starts to describe her attempted solutions. These include comforting, which is keeping with the 'you need to relax' message, and enhancing her confidence with the message of 'Believe in yourself').

Coach: *Does that help?*

Michelle: No, not really.

Coach: *It doesn't help at all? It helps a little? Or does it make matters worse?*

Michelle: Hmmm, I should know, shouldn't I? I know it's not helping enough. I've been so focused on comforting her, helping her, that I haven't given it much thought. How odd!

Coach: *Not really, we get so caught up in doing something to support our loved ones that we don't give much thought to what it is that we are doing and whether it is helpful ... or not.* (Normalizing but at the same time seeding the idea that the logical solution is the problem.)

Michelle: Hmmm. I need to look into that.

Coach: *That would be a good idea. It will give me a lot of important infor-
              mation to better help Jenny. Until our next session then, continue
              doing what you're doing. I'd prefer you didn't make any changes
              just yet. Simply observe how Jenny responds to you being there in
              that specific way of comforting and empowering her without
              changing your ways yet. Would that be OK?*

Michelle followed suggestions to a tee up until a couple of days before our
next session.

Coach: *So, Michelle, what did you notice since our last session?*

Michelle: I realized that the more I stayed home, the more she would act out
              crying. So, when I was at home for a long period of time, I would
              pretend I needed to run errands, I would leave for a while and it
              seemed to work. She seemed calmer. I also had a talk with her and
              told her I love her and how proud I am of her and that won't change
              … no matter what.

Coach: *That's an important message we all need to hear, no matter what
              our age.*

Michelle: Yes, and I have to say that's not how I used to be with my other
              children.

Coach: *No?*

Michelle: No, it saddens me to say that I was very demanding. I was always by
              their side, ensuring they had everything they needed but I was act-
              ing more like a general (becomes tearful herself). I have been in
              therapy this last year and realized how strict I was. Loving but way
              too demanding. I wouldn't accept anything less than success and I
              would not allow my kids to even think about not making the cut. It
              was not an option. There was a lot of guilt when I realized what I
              was doing and I have changed my ways.

Coach: *Good for you, so the talk you had with Jenny would not have been
              one you'd have with her older siblings when they were preparing
              for their university exams.*

Michelle: No, not at all. And that's what I want to mention. This is really
              important.

Coach: *OK.*

Michelle: She probably had the worst sobbing spell up to date following that
              talk. I have never seen her in such a state. There was nothing I could
              do to comfort her and … I became a bit of my old self … I demanded
              she stopped. I told her I will not accept self-pity, that she has no
              choice but to succeed and told her to go back to her room and do
              what needs to be done.

Coach: *How did that work out?* (Assessing the spontaneous solution attempt.)

Michelle: Surprisingly well. She got angry and slammed the door behind her but
              when I checked in on her later – I didn't ask if she was feeling OK but

made her some toast and gave her some orange juice – she seemed calmer and more focused. And there was a test the next day and she improved her scores. These last two days have been better but that's not the kind of mum I want to be. (Any suggestions must fit with her viewing herself as a better version of the mum she used to be.)

Coach: *Well, it seems that when you comfort her, try to relax her or enhance her confidence, it backfires. And the moment you stopped and simply demanded that she outperforms herself, things improved.*

Michelle: True. I was thinking the other day that it may be that she witnessed how I used to handle matters with my other kids when she was young and she is more accustomed to that.

Coach: *It is possible. Would you be able to keep the change? And show your love and affection in various other ways … just like popping in her room with freshly squeezed orange juice and some toast, baking her favourite food, going out for a walk with her, etc., just to test your theory and see whether her mood and grades go up.*

Michelle: Just until June.

Coach: *Yes, and when this is over, you can have a chat with her and set things straight so she'll have no qualms about the kind of mum you are and continue to be. We can talk about that when the time comes.*

Michelle called a week later saying that Jenny's scores returned to her usual 90s. She called again two weeks later to let me know that Jenny is anxious about the results but also hopeful. She wanted some advice about the 'talk' she had just had. Jenny confessed that the more her mother comforted her and told her she was loved regardless of her final performance, the more she felt that she had given up on her. Jenny remembers her mum being demanding with her older siblings and the change towards her was interpreted as Michelle not believing in her as much as she believed in the others, and that she wasn't expecting much from her.

This is an example of how insight can come after change, which was important since time was not on our side. This case shows how you cannot foretell the direction you will take with each client. This is definitely not the kind of suggestions I would give to any parent. However, the exploration of attempted solutions pointed to what needed to be done.

The man just won't stop! The more I try to stop him, the more he continues

Remember Michael? He has been finding it difficult to deal with a certain well-mannered colleague who repeatedly second-guesses his input during meetings. He has clarified the problem to the coach and set the desired goal of finding a way to minimize the colleague's behaviour. He describes how he tries to cope with the situation.

Coach:	*And what do you do when that happens?*
Michael:	What do I do?
Coach:	*Yes, when we are faced with a difficulty, our first instinct is to do something to help ourselves.*
Michael:	(Nods.)
Coach:	*How do you try to handle the situation?*
Michael:	I try to hide my stress – there's no way I'll give him the pleasure of knowing that he has any impact on me – and I avoid eye contact with him, I concentrate on others, hoping it will make me less of a target.
Coach:	*Has that been working?*
Michael:	No.
Coach:	*No?*
Michael:	No, not at all.
Coach:	*Well, what you do is the logical thing to do … but logic doesn't seem to be making the cut, does it?* (Seeding the idea of an 'illogical' direction at a later stage.)
Michael:	No.
Coach:	*Over time, have things improved, remained stable or taken a turn for the worse?*
Michael:	It's got out of hand … he just won't stop.
Coach:	*I see … Am I correct to say that trying to remain calm and keeping a low profile as to avoid undue attention has not only been unhelpful but has escalated matters? Am I getting it right?* (One-down position.)
Michael:	Yes.
Coach:	*Anything else you have tried?*
Michael:	Before that, in the beginning, I confronted him and told him to stop undermining me.
Coach:	*And?*
Michael:	He denied it, he talked about how, in a team, everyone contributes and accused me of not being a good sport, which got me angry, but he is very soft-spoken so I ended up being the one looking unprofessional.
Coach:	*I see. Anything else you've tried?*
Michael:	No, but it's got to the point that I'm contemplating making a U-turn on my way to work and calling in sick. If this doesn't change, I'm thinking of looking for another job, but I don't want to call it quits yet.
Coach:	*I'm getting the picture … Can I share some of my observations about the ways you've tried to change his behaviour?* (One-down position.)
Michael:	Sure.
Coach:	*They may seem different to you, but they are actually quite similar.* (Proceeding towards finding the common theme.)
Michael:	In what way?

Coach:	*Well, both share the same message you are trying to convey. Both solutions attempt to get him to …* (Pausing intentionally to see if he can fill in the blank and provide the answer himself.)
Michael:	Stop.
Coach:	*Exactly. The message is 'You must stop!'*
Michael:	Basically, yes.
Coach:	*And the more you are trying to stop him, the more he …* (Waiting for Michael to answer.)
Michael:	… continues.
Coach:	*Yes, the more he continues … And although it makes sense to send the message 'Stop trying to feel important and valued at my expense', it hasn't helped. It's got worse. Does that seem about right to you?* (Examining the effectiveness of attempted solutions with first reframing seeds about the intent of feeling important behind the colleague's behaviour. I added 'at my expense' to the intent as I felt it was a bit too early not to and I anticipated that if I didn't add it, he probably would.)
Michael:	I guess.
Coach:	*Well, when you want to arrive at a certain place and you realize you're driving on the wrong road, what do you do?* (Using his previous image of driving to work and being tempted to make a U-turn and go back home.)
Michael:	Get off that road.
Coach:	*Yes, you get off that road and onto another one, don't you?*
Michael:	I see, I need to get on another road.
Coach:	*But here's the catch. Not any other road. It must a road heading in another direction or you'll still end up in the wrong place.* (Seeding the illogical solution that is soon to come.)
Michael:	(Nods.)
Coach:	*Both the roads you've taken have been heading in the direction of 'Stop it! Stop trying to show your value! Stop trying to feel important!' and that hasn't been working, despite it being the most logical thing to do. What would be another direction to take here?*
Michael:	To bring it on.
Coach:	*Yes, bring it on. Invite it instead. What do you think will happen if you invite his feedback before he initiates it at the next meeting? And when he does, thank him for adding strength to your proposal and making it look better. Maybe you could thank him privately after the meeting. You could say something like: 'I'd like to thank you. I've been getting pretty good feedback about my ideas as a result of your input. I apologize for not understanding how helpful you have been. I'm counting on your input at our next meetings.'*

We laid out a plan that was feasible for Michael and refined it in the next couple of sessions depending on how the colleague responded. Michael's colleague was initially perplexed by the change but seemed more than happy to show off his input. However, after a while he no longer appreciated being repeatedly asked about what he thought and started to cut back on his behaviour.

Forget about that! There's something else I need you to help me with

Stacey works in the family business that her father built from nothing half a century ago and now employs over 30 people. Her presenting complaint concerns her father's disrespect and distrust in her abilities. He is in his mid-seventies and is not keen to hand over responsibilities, let alone to consider succession.

Coach: *We had a brief chat over the phone when we scheduled the appointment. So I have a rudimentary idea but obviously I'll need your help to get a clearer picture. What prompted you to pick up the phone and come in today?*

Stacey: Yes, I mentioned on the phone that I work in the family business and my office is next to dad's. He built the business by working hard and putting in very long hours ... I don't remember him being at home much or being part of my life growing up.

Coach: *And you are now working together, offices side by side, and you get to see him every day.*

Stacey: I assure you there's no fun in that! There's never a good word coming out of that man's mouth. He'll always find something to criticize and put you down.

Coach: *Can you help me understand better by giving me an example what criticizing and putting you down looks like?*

Stacey: What it would look like?

Coach: *If you had a video of an example, what would I see and hear that would make me say 'Oh yes, he's criticizing and putting her down'.* (Getting a behavioural account of the problem.)

Stacey: Well, a couple of days ago I struck a deal with a supplier – I won't bore you with the details – but I'll tell you that in the end it turned out to be a good one – and when my dad found out, he came storming in the office calling me an idiot and incompetent. He's old school so he's crude and doesn't think twice before opening his mouth. It's his way or no way. No self-control, not even when there's staff around.

Coach: *It wasn't just the two of you?*

Stacey: No, but he lashes at everyone so they are used to it.

Coach: *Can you offer another example?*

Stacey: It's more or less similar behaviour. Name calling, telling me that he wants to retire but how could he retire knowing I'm not good enough to fill in his shoes. He'll assign me some work and casually remind me not to screw up but, even if I don't screw up, he'll find some flaw in my results.

Coach: *Ok, I'm getting the picture. What would be a sign of change? What would you like to see happen that will tell you that things are getting better?* (Clarifying desired change.)

Stacey: Well, I called you because I don't want to feel so impacted by what he does, I want to feel calmer and confident despite his behaviour.

Coach: *And by managing to feel calmer and more confident, what would you be doing differently? What would Stacey do and say on that video that would be different?* (Gaining a clearer depiction of the desired change.)

Stacey: Well, I wouldn't snap back, which is what I usually do and things spiral out of control. I would let him calm down first and then get over the facts with him.

Coach: *OK, what else?*

Stacey: What else? Other than giving him the facts, nothing really ... hmmm, basically I'll be doing less than what I usually do.

Coach: *What do you usually do?*

Stacey: Well, I urge him to calm down, remind him that we're at work, not at home. I tell him that he is old school and that things have changed since half a century ago, that if he could just listen he'd see that I can actually bring the business up to date. I try to somehow get him to see the work I do in a better light.

Coach: *So you try to improve the situation by asking him to calm down, by defending your work, by putting him down and then trying to show him the evidence of good work. Would that be right?*

Stacey: I'm becoming like my dad, that hurts!

Coach: *We tend to pick up behaviours we're accustomed to without being aware of them. At least, up until we become aware of them.* (Presupposition that it will change.)

Stacey: (Nods.)

Coach: *And in your case, it's an attempt to get him to acknowledge your work.* (Positive intent behind behaviour.)

Stacey: It is. It would be nice if I could get a good word out of him, some vote of confidence.

Coach: *It would be nice even if it were any boss, let alone your father.*

Stacey: (Nods.)

Coach: *Anything else you do to help with the situation, other than defending your work and seeking some acknowledgement?*

Stacey: No, it's the same video every time, I guess.

Coach: *And it hasn't been helpful in any small way?*

Stacey: No.

Coach: *So, you try to deal with the situation by defending yourself and by getting him to acknowledge your work. And things are getting worse?* (Examining effectiveness of attempted solutions.)

Stacey: Yes.

Coach: *What you've been doing is guided by logic: 'Look at my work and you'll see that I'm right.'*

Stacey: Exactly. Am I asking too much?

Coach: *Who doesn't want to feel acknowledged? Yet this logical way has led things astray.*

Stacey: (Nods.)

Coach: *I wonder if you have any ideas about a different kind of direction we can take. Sometimes, we may need to go in the opposite direction and stop that video from replaying.*

Stacey: Not really. I certainly don't want to agree that I'm incompetent. (Gives an idea about her position.)

Coach: *No, not at all. I do have an idea – it is different from what you've been doing and it won't be what you expect. You'll probably surprise your dad because he won't be expecting it either, but I'm not sure if you're up for it yet. I don't want to be going too fast …* (Pre-empting and pre-supposition.)

Stacey: Don't act like my dad asking me if I'm up for it!

Coach: *I wouldn't dare.* (Laughter.) *I'm glad you're ready for it.*

Rather than defending herself, it was suggested she would invite his input. It was important to pay attention to the words used so that Stacey was not accepting incompetence but showing respect for her father's experience and mentoring potential. Asking 'What would you suggest with your experience that I did?' or 'What would have been a better alternative?' before her father would have a chance to criticize her changed the familiar solution pattern. After two weeks, Stacey confirmed that there were positive changes.

Coach: *What's different since last time?*

Stacey: It actually worked. I can tell when he's just about to start criticizing so I ask for his feedback before he does. It's like disarming him. I have taken it a bit further, though.

Coach: *Have you?*

Stacey: I could see the satisfaction in him when I ask for his suggestions and it struck me that he just wants to feel important.

Coach: *Don't we all …*

Stacey: When I see him running late for a meeting or when he's very busy, I might intentionally ask for some of his tips or ideas for which I know he has no time to discuss … And he usually mumbles and tells me that he can't be telling me what to do all the time and that I need to take more initiative!

Coach: *I see. You've certainly got the idea right, but you may want to slow down a bit. I want you and your dad to have the time to process all this change. Could you hold on from initiating any further changes yet … just for a little while?* (Paradox of going slow and presupposition.). *OK?*

Stacey: OK.

Stacey was also warned of the possibility that her father might occasionally revert to his old behaviour, and of the importance that she did not. She was also encouraged to defend herself once during the following week, just to check how he'd respond, which is similar to planning a relapse. In a following session, Stacey was asked whether changes had been maintained.

Coach: *What has changed since last time?*

Stacey: Things are going pretty well but forget about dad. That's not why I'm here today. There's something else I need you to help me with.

Coach: *OK, what is the problem?* (Working with the presenting complaint even when it changes.)

Stacey: I can't get myself to wake up in the morning and arrive at work on time. I've been realizing how bad it is. How can I demand respect when I'm like a child who knows that dad will go to work first and take care of any pressing matters and then I'll show up when I manage to drag myself out of bed?

Coach: *What time do you have to be at work?*

Stacey: At 9am. It's not early and I try to get up at 8am but it doesn't work out.

Coach: *So, your goal would be to get up at 8am, go through your morning routine and leave home at what time?* (Clarifying desired change and setting up first goal.)

Stacey: 8:30 would be OK.

Coach: *So, waking up at 8, leaving home at 8:30 and arriving at the office by 9. Would that be right?*

Stacey: Yes, that's the plan.

Coach: *Sounds good. And how have you been trying to get up at 8?*

Stacey: I set the alarm; it doesn't work.

Coach: *You don't wake up?*

Stacey: No, I do wake up. I fall back to sleep, even if I reset it. I'll wake up and soon fall back to sleep. I am unable to remain awake.

Coach: *So, when you do wake up, do you remain lying down?*

Stacey: No, I sit up.

Coach: *And then what? Can you describe what happens after you sit up? Step by step?* (Exploring solution attempts.)

Stacey: I sit up. And I do relaxation exercises.

Coach: *Relaxation?*

Stacey: Yes, I follow a relaxation routine to ward off stress about work and dad. I just try to relax before I start my day.

Coach: *You try to relax?*

Stacey: Yes.

Coach: *Can you tell me more about that please? What kind of relaxation do you follow?*

Stacey: Breathing work that I've learned from yoga.

Coach: *Does it relax you?*

Stacey: Very much so.

Coach: *So, you've just woken up, still half asleep and you try to get ready for work by relaxing in bed. What do you think relaxation in bed leads to?* (Assessing solution attempt.)

Stacey: Oh!

Trying to relax and cope with the anticipatory stress while in bed would put her back to sleep. Several months later, a follow-up call showed that Stacey had maintained her gains, got to work on time and dealt with her father's behaviour in a better way. Her father still snaps at her every now and then, but considerably less than before and she's OK with it. That means there's no complaint and, thus, no problem. And she still does her relaxation exercises but at a different time of day.

8 Are You Part of the Problem?

I was recently contacted by a company concerned about a rise in employee negative sentiment. The conversation with staff revealed that the dent in employee satisfaction and work culture followed a manager-as-coach training over six months ago. The following complaint was indicative of the reigning sentiment:

> 'Before our supervisors attended coach training, they would actually try to help when you needed it. Now when you seek guidance, they'll ask 'What would you do?'. When you tell them that you don't know, they'll say, 'If you did know, what would you do?' and when you tell them again that you don't know, they just keep on repeating the same question, 'If you did know, what would you do?'

Obviously, this is a misapplied ask-don't-tell stance. An attempt to empower staff to self-initiate changes in behaviour and come up with their own decisions about their next step ended up leaving staff feeling unsupported and hung out to dry. This does not mean that an ask-don't-tell approach is by default the wrong way to go but it does mean that it is, just like many other tactics we choose based on our approach, an attempt to serve our coachees' goals. And solution attempts, as we have discussed, can complicate the problem or create problems where there were none.

The strategic approach is an interactive approach. It is how we interact with our problems and how we interact with other people that is the heart of the matter. Understandably, the interaction between coach and coachee is no exception and this also needs to be scrutinized. Just as we assess what other people are doing or not doing in an effort to help our coachees so that we can discern whether they are inadvertently nourishing the problem, strategic coaches also assess their own 'tactics'. They are mindful of the fact that they embody a coachee's attempted solution.

As coachees employ a coach in their effort to reach their goals, it is recommended that coaches adopt a reflective practice and, in doing so, constantly reflect on their own helping efforts. This entails stepping out of one's pre-existing frame of reference concerning change. It entails both challenging and assessing the impact of preconceived beliefs and practices, as well as being observed as well as an observer throughout the session; a process widely adopted by professionals to evaluate their practices in qualitative research to validate research procedures (Mortari 2015, Taylor 2020). The goal is to move from reflection-on-action to reflection-in-action (Schön 1987, Mortari 2015). Strategically speaking, that means to progress from reflecting after implementing a solution and observing its results to reflecting while attempting to apply a helping tactic. Strategic reflection, in particular, involves reflecting on *how* we attempt to help our coachees, and the outcome of those efforts in relation to the coachee's goals. The objective is to identify and break our own faulty patterns.

In the absence of changes after a number of coaching sessions, the strategic model recommends referring the client elsewhere for a simple reason. If coaches continue doing more of the same that's not working, they are contributing to the vicious cycle of problem maintenance and becoming an accomplice to the problem (Nardone and Salvini 2007). Could we inadvertently become part of the problem-maintenance cycle in our attempts to help our coachees? In order to avoid becoming the problem, there follows a number of strategic reflective questions that will hopefully provide plenty of food for thought.

- What is our mindset about change? Can it come about briefly (quickly) or does it need to be a long-term process? How do we approach change when it occurs briefly? Do we expect it to be short-lived? How does that affect our practice?
- How can we use the attempted solutions theory to elevate our work and avoid unintended consequences?
- Do we reflect on our attempts to assist our coachees during sessions and their outcomes? When results are not what was expected, do we fall prey to one of the three maladaptive solution types?
- Are we attempting to create second-order change when first-order change would suffice?
- Could our attempts to help be contributing to problem maintenance?
- What are the possible problem-maintaining properties of a consistent non-directive stance?
- When does an insistent ask-don't-tell approach end up crushing a client's confidence and motivation rather than empower them?
- When does an insistent directive stance or generous offering of advice become a faulty solution pattern that disempowers the coachee and minimizes their independence?
- When do long-term or frequent coaching contracts become part of the problem-maintenance cycle?
- When does focusing on negative affect amplify the emotions we're trying to process and when does focusing on solutions reduce the feeling of being understood and supported?

- Are we attempting to help coachees by doing more of the same, which got them stuck in the first place and caused them to ask for our help?

Regardless of our coaching approach, the strategic model emphasizes that any solution attempt carries a risk of turning a mere difficulty into a full-blown problem and feeding a vicious cycle of problem maintenance. We cannot foretell whether what facilitated one coachee's success will complicate someone else's problem. In order to better serve our clients, the strategic model strongly encourages being mindful, throughout our sessions, of the fact that our attempted solutions could go both ways. Maintaining manoeuvrability will give us the wiggle room or flexibility to make the necessary modifications to how we are dealing with our coachee's problem so that we do not become part of the problem.

Brief strategic coaches see client problems as maintained by their attempted solutions. The main goal is to break the problem-maintaining cycle by identifying clients' well-intended but faulty attempted solutions and replace them with new more effective, yet often counterintuitive, ones. Fisch and Schlanger (1999: 36) succinctly express the basic thrust of the approach: *We treat solutions, not problems.*

Our own included.

References

Amini, R.L. and Woolley, S.R. (2011) First-session competency: the brief strategic therapy scale-1, *Journal of Marital and Family Therapy*, 37(2): 209–22.

Andreas, S. (1991) *Virginia Satir: The Patterns of her Magic*. Moab, UT: Real People Press.

Andreas, S. (n.d.) Verbal implication. Milton H. Erickson Foundation. Available at: www.erickson-foundation.org/verbal-implication

Argyris, C. and Schön, D. (1978) *Organizational Learning: A Theory of Action Perspective*. Reading, MA: Addison-Wesley Publishing.

Armatas, A. (2009) Coaching hypnosis: integrating hypnotic strategies and principles in coaching, *International Coaching Psychology Review*, 4(2): 172–81.

Armatas, A. (2010) *Breaking the pattern: when the solution is the problem*. Paper presented at the First International Congress of Coaching Psychology, London.

Armatas, A. (2011) Suggestive techniques in coaching, *Coaching: An International Journal of Theory, Research and Practice*, 4(1): 32–41.

Armatas, A. (2015) Improving employee wellbeing: the role of coaching psychology, in A.S. Antoniou (ed.), *Current Perspectives in Occupational Health Psychology, Volume B*. Nicosia: Broken Hills Publishers.

Armatas, A. (2019) Breaking the pattern in teams: when the solution is the problem, in D. Clutterbuck, J. Gannon, S. Hayes, I. Iordanou, K. Lowe and D. MacKie (eds), *The Practitioner's Handbook of Team Coaching*. Abingdon: Routledge.

Armatas, A. (2020) *When solutions become the problem: a brief strategic perspective*. Paper presented at the 16th Annual Coaching and Mentoring Research Conference, Oxford Brookes University, Oxford.

Armatas, A. (2021) How the solution becomes the problem: The performance solution that backfired at Microsoft, *SAGE Business Cases*. Available at: https://www.doi.org/10.4135/9781529759075

Bannink, F. and Jackson, P.Z. (2011) Positive psychology and solution focus: looking at similarities and differences, *Interaction: The Journal of Solution Focus in Organizations*, 3(1): 8–20.

Bateson, G., Jackson, D.D., Haley, J. and Weakland, J. (1956) Toward a theory of schizophrenia, *Behavioral Science*, 1(4): 251–54.

Bateson, G., Jackson, D.D., Haley, J. and Weakland, J.H. (1963) A note on the double bind – 1962, *Family Process*, 2(1): 154–61.

Bavelas, J.B., Chovil, N., Lawrie, D. and Wade, A. (1992) Interactive gestures, *Discourse Processes*, 15: 469–89.

Berg, I.K. (1989) Of visitors, complainants, and customers: is there really such a thing as resistance?, *Family Therapy Networker*, 13(1): 21–25.

Berg, I.K. and Miller, S.D. (1992) *Working with the Problem Drinker: A Solution-Oriented Approach*. New York: W.W. Norton.

Brown, P. (1997) Hypnosis and metaphor, in J. Rhue, S. Lynn and I. Kirsch (eds), *Handbook of Clinical Hypnosis*. Washington, DC: American Psychological Association.

Cade, B. (1987) Brief/strategic approaches to therapy: a commentary, *Australian and New Zealand Journal of Family Therapy*, 8: 37–44.

Cade, B. and O'Hanlon W.H. (1993) *A Brief Guide to Brief Therapy*. New York: W.W. Norton.

Cade, B. (2001) Building alternative futures: the solution-focused approach, in S. Cullari (ed.), *Counselling and Psychotherapy*. Needham Heights, MA: Allyn and Bacon.

Cade, B.W. (2013) Unpredictability and change: a holographic metaphor, in G.R. Weeks (ed.), *Promoting Change Through Paradoxical Therapy*. Chevy Chase, MD: International Psychotherapy Institute.

Caniato, D. and Skorjanec, B. (2002) The role of brief strategic therapy on the outcome of gastric banding, *Obesity Surgery*, 12: 666–71.

Carr, A. (1998) Michael White's narrative therapy, *Contemporary Family Therapy*, 20(4): 485–503.

Carratala, E., Vilaregut, A., Schlanger, K. and Günther, C. (2016) Problem solving brief therapy: a case conducted by John Weakland, *Revista de Psicoterapia*, 27(104): 217–32.

Castelnuovo, G., Manzoni, G.M., Villa, V., Cesa, G.L. and Molinari, E. (2011) Brief strategic therapy vs cognitive behavioral therapy for the inpatient and telephone-based outpatient treatment of binge eating disorder: the STRATOB randomized controlled clinical trial, *Clinical Practice and Epidemiology in Mental Health*, 7: 29–37.

Chubb, H. (1982) Strategic brief therapy in a clinical setting, *Psychotherapy: Theory, Research and Practice*, 19(2): 160–65.

Clark, D.A. (2013) Cognitive restructuring, in S.G. Hofmann (ed.), *The Wiley Handbook of Cognitive Behavioral Therapy, Volume 1*. New York: Wiley.

Coats, E.J., Janoff-Bulman, R. and Alpert, N. (1996) Approach versus avoidance goals: differences in self-evaluation and well-being, *Personality and Social Psychology Bulletin*, 22(10): 1057–67.

Coyne, J.C. (1985) Toward a theory of frames and reframing: the social nature of frames, *Journal of Marital and Family Therapy*, 11(4): 337–44.

Coyne, J.C. and Segal, L. (1982) A brief, strategic interactional approach to psychotherapy, in J. Anchin and D.J. Kiesler (eds), *Handbook of Interpersonal Psychotherapy*. New York: Pergamon.

Coyne, J.C. and Pepper, C.M. (1998) The therapeutic alliance in brief strategic therapy, in J.D. Safran and J.C. Muran (eds), *The Therapeutic Alliance in Brief Psychotherapy*. Washington, DC: American Psychological Association.

Craigie, F.C. (1985) Therapeutic homework: the use of behavioral assignments in office counseling, *Journal of Family Practice*, 20(1): 66–71.

de Shazer, S. (1985) *Keys to Solution in Brief Therapy*. New York: W.W. Norton.

de Shazer, S., Berg, I.K., Lipchik, E., Nunnally, E., Molnar, A., Gingerich, W. and Weiner-Davis, M. (1986) Brief therapy: focused solution development, *Family Process*, 25(2): 207–21.

de Shazer, S. (1994) *Words Were Originally Magic*. New York: W.W. Norton.

Dormaar, J.M., Dijkman, C.I. and de Vries, M.W. (1989) Consensus in patient-therapist interactions: a measure of the therapeutic relationship related to outcome, *Psychotherapy and Psychosomatics*, 51(2): 69–76.

Dryden, W. (2019) *Single-Session Coaching and One-at-a-Time Coaching*. Abingdon: Routledge

Dryden, W. (2020) Single-session one-at-a-time therapy: a personal approach, *Australian and New Zealand Journal of Family Therapy*, 41: 283–301.

Duncan, B.L. and Solovey, A.D. (1989) Strategic-brief therapy: an insight-oriented approach, *Journal of Marital and Family Therapy*, 15(1): 1–9.

Duncan, B.L., Parks, M.B. and Rusk, G.S. (1990) Strategic eclecticism: a technical alternative for eclectic psychotherapy, *Psychotherapy*, 27(7): 568–77.

Duterme, C. (2004) 'Translating' Palo Alto approach in the companies' consultancy, *Brief Strategic and Systemic Therapy European Review*, 1: 185–92.

Eisenberg, J. and Wahrman, O. (1994) Brief strategic therapy in a child community clinic: a follow up report, *Israel Journal of Psychiatry and Related Sciences*, 31(1): 37–40.

Erickson, M.H. and Rossi, E.L. (1979) *Hypnotherapy: An Exploratory Handbook*. New York: Irvington Publishers.

Erickson, M.H. (2009; original work published 1959) Further clinical techniques of hypnosis: utilization techniques. 1959, *American Journal of Clinical Hypnosis*, 51(4): 341–62.

Eubanks, R.A. (2002) The MRI reflecting team: an integrated approach, *Journal of Systemic Therapies*, 21(1): 10–19.

Evans, F.B. (1996) *Harry Stack Sullivan: Interpersonal Theory and Psychotherapy*. London: Routledge.

Fisch, R., Weakland, J.H. and Segal, L. (1982) *The Tactics of Change: Doing Therapy Briefly*. San Francisco, CA: Jossey-Bass.

Fisch, R. and Schlanger, K. (1999) *Brief Therapy with Intimidating Cases: Changing the Unchangeable*. San Francisco, CA: Jossey-Bass.

Fisch, R. (2004) So, what have you done lately? MRI brief therapy, *Journal of Systemic Therapies*, 23(4): 4–10.

Flaskas, C. (1992) Reframing, framing and frameworks ... can we be framed?, *Journal of Family Therapy*, 14(2): 171–75.

Fölscher-Kingwill, B. and Terblanche, N. (2019) The role of coaching and coach language in clients' language and individual change, *International Journal of Evidence Based Coaching and Mentoring*, 17(2): 158–73.

Fraser, J.S. (1995) Process, problems and solutions in brief therapy, *Journal of Marital and Family Therapy*, 21(3): 265–79.

Fraser, J.S. and Solovey, A.D. (2007) *Second-Order Change in Psychotherapy: The Golden Thread that Unifies Effective Treatments*. Washington, DC: American Psychological Association.

Fullen, C.T. (2019) The therapeutic alliance in a single session: a conversation analysis, *Journal of Systemic Therapies*, 38(4): 45–61.

Geary, B.B. (2001) Assessment in Ericksonian hypnosis and psychotherapy, in B.B. Geary and J.K. Zeig (eds), *The Handbook of Ericksonian Psychotherapy*. Phoenix, AZ: The Milton H. Erickson Foundation Press.

Geary, B.B. and Zeig, J.K. (eds) (2001) *The Handbook of Ericksonian Psychotherapy*. Phoenix, AZ: The Milton H. Erickson Foundation Press.

Georgiou, Y.S. and Fotiou, A. (2019) Burnout and coping strategies, *Montenegrin Journal of Sports Science and Medicine*, 8(2): 33–38.

Gibney, P. (2006) The double bind theory: still crazy-making after all these years, *Psychotherapy in Australia*, 12(3): 48–55.

Gill, L. (1999) *How to Work with Just About Anyone: A 3-Step Solution for Getting Difficult People to Change*. New York: Fireside.

Gneezy, U. and Rustichini, A. (2000) A fine is a price, *The Journal of Legal Studies*, XXIX: 1–18.

Goldenberg, I., Stanton, N. and Goldenberg, H. (2016) *Family Therapy: An Overview*, 9th edn. Boston, MA: Cengage Learning.

Gonçalves, M.M., Matos, M. and Santos, A. (2009) Narrative therapy and the nature of 'innovative moments' in the construction of change, *Journal of Constructivist Psychology*, 22(1): 1–23.

Gonzalez, M.T., Estrada, B. and O'Hanlon, B. (2011) Possibilities and solutions: the differences that make a difference, *International Journal of Hispanic Psychology*, 3(2): 185–200.

Gordon, D. and Meyers-Anderson, M. (1981) *Phoenix: Therapeutic Patterns of M.H. Erickson*. Cupertino, CA: Meta Publications.

Graham, G.H. (2003) Role preparation in brief strategic therapy: the welcome letter, *Journal of Systemic Therapies*, 22(1): 3–14.

Grinder, J. and Bandler, R. (1982) *Reframing: Neurolinguistic Programming and the Transformation of Meaning*. Moab, UT: Real People Press.

Hale, D. and Frusha, C.V. (2016) MRI brief therapy: a tried and true systemic approach, *Journal of Systemic Therapies*, 35(2): 14–24.

Haley, J. (1973) *Uncommon Therapy: The Psychiatric Techniques of Milton H. Erickson, M.D.* New York: W.W. Norton.

Haley, J. (1976) *Problem-Solving Therapy: New Strategies for Effective Family Therapy.* San Francisco, CA: Jossey-Bass.

Haley, J. and Richeport-Haley, M. (2003) *The Art of Strategic Therapy*. New York: Routledge.

Haley, J. (2013; original work published 1993) *Jay Haley on Milton H. Erickson*. New York: Routledge.

Hammond, D.C. (1990) *Handbook of Hypnotic Suggestions and Metaphors*. New York: W.W. Norton.

Hart, C.L. and Randell, J.A. (2006) Ironic effects of mental control in problem solving: evidence for the implementation of ineffective strategies, *American Journal of Academic Research*, 2(1): 40–45.

Havens, R. (2003) *The Wisdom of Milton H. Erickson, The Complete Volume*. Carmarthen: Crown House Publishing.

Healing, S. and Bavelas, J.B. (2011) Can questions lead to change? An analogue experiment, *Journal of Systemic Therapies*, 30(4): 30–47.

Heath, A.W. and Atkinson, B.J. (1989) Solutions attempted and considered: broadening assessment in brief therapy, *Journal of Strategic and Systemic Therapies*: 8: 2–3.

Held, B.S. (1986) The relationship between individual psychologies and strategic/systematic therapies reconsidered, in D.E. Efron (ed.), *Journeys: Expansion of the Strategic-Systemic Therapies*. New York: Brunner-Mazel.

Horigian, V., Robbins, N. and Szapocznik, J. (2004) Brief strategic family therapy, *Brief Strategic and Systemic Therapy European Review*, 1: 251–71.

Hoyt, M.F. and Talmon, M. (eds) (2014) *Capturing the Moment: Single Session Therapy and Walk-in Services*. Carmarthen: Crown House Publishing.

Hoyt, M.F. (2019) Strategic therapies: roots and branches, *Journal of Systemic Therapies*, 38(1): 30–43.

Israelstam, K. (1988) Contrasting four major family therapy paradigms: implications for family therapy training, *Journal of Family Therapy*, 10: 179–96.

Jacobson, A. (1983) Empowering the client in strategic therapy, *Journal of Strategic and Systemic Therapies, Theme Issue: Theoretical and Practical Issues and Applications of Strategic and Systemic Therapies*, 2: 77–88.

Jensen, T.R., Hòyer, T.R. and Spaten, O.M. (2018) Narrative therapy and narrative coaching: distinctions and similarities, *The Danish Journal of Coaching Psychology*, 7(1): 27–38.

Kanter, J. (2013) Helping, healing and interpreting: Sullivan, the Interpersonal School and clinical social work, *Journal of Social Work*, 27(3): 273–87.

Kaslow, F.W. (2007) A brief history of the field of family psychology and therapy, in F. Shapiro, F.W. Kaslow and L. Maxfield (eds), *Handbook of EMDR and Family Therapy Processes*. Hoboken, NJ: John Wiley.

Keeney, H. and Keeney, B. (2012) What is systemic about systemic therapy? Therapy models muddle embodied systemic practice, *Journal of Systemic Practice*, 31(1): 22–37.

Klaij, K. (2016) Jay Haley: pioneer in strategic family therapy, *Psychotherapia*, 2(177): 17–28.

Leeds-Hurwitz, W. (2005) The natural history approach: Bateson's legacy, *Cybernetics and Human Knowing*, 12(1–2): 137–46.

Leeds-Hurwitz, W. (2016) Social construction, in P. Moy (ed.) *Oxford Bibliographies in Communication*. New York: Oxford University Press.

Locke, E.A. and Latham, G.P. (2002) Building a practically useful theory of goal setting and task motivation: a 35-year odyssey, *American Psychologist*, 57(9): 705–17.

Locke, E.A. and Latham, G.P. (2006) New directions in goal-setting theory, *Current Directions in Psychological Science*, 15(5): 265–68.

Madanes, C. (1991) Strategic family therapy, in A.S. Gurman and D.P. Kniskern (eds), *Handbook of Family Therapy, Volume 2*. New York: Brunner-Mazel.

Marsen, S. (2006) How to mean without saying: presupposition and implication revisited, *Semiotica*, 160: 243–63.

Mattila, A. (2001) *Seeing Things in a New Light: Reframing in Therapeutic Conversation*. Helsinki: Helsinki University Press.

McKergow, M. (2013) Fifty years of the interactional view – an interview with Janet Bavelas, *InterAction*, 5: 92–116.

Morgan, J.H. (2014) The interpersonal therapy of Harry Stack Sullivan: remembering the legacy, *Journal of Psychology and Psychotherapy*, 4(6): 162.

Mortari, L. (2015). Reflectivity in research practice: An overview of different perspectives. *International Journal of Qualitative Methods*, 1-9. https://doi.org/10.1177/1609406915618045

Mozdzierz, G.J., Macchitelli, F.J. and Lisiecki, J. (1976) The paradox in psychotherapy: an Adlerian perspective, *Journal of Individual Psychology*, 32(2): 169–84.

Murphy, J.J. and Duncan, B.L. (2007) *Brief Interventions for School Problems: Outcome Informed. Strategies*, 2nd edn. New York: Guilford Press.

Nardone, G. (2004). Notes on brief strategic therapy, *Brief Strategic and Systemic Therapy European Review*, 1: 65–73.

Nardone, G. and Portelli, C. (2005) *Knowing Through Changing: The Evolution of Brief Strategic Therapy*. Carmarthen: Crown House Publishing.

Nardone, G. and Watzlawick, P. (2005) *Brief Strategic Therapy: Philosophy, Techniques and Research*. Lanham, MD: Jason Aronson.

Nardone, G. and Salvini, A. (2007) *The Strategic Dialogue*. London: Routledge.

Nichols, M. and Schwartz, R. (2005) *Family Therapy: Concepts and Methods*, 7th edn. New York: Prentice Hall.

O'Hanlon, B. (2000) *Do One Thing Different: Ten Simple Ways to Change Your Life*. New York: William Morrow.

O'Hanlon, B. and Weiner-Davis, M. (2003; original work published 1989) *In Search of Solutions: A New Direction in Psychotherapy*. New York: W.W. Norton.

Perrotta, G. (2020) The strategic clinical model in psychotherapy: theoretical and practical profiles, *Journal of Addiction and Adolescent Behavior*, 3(1). doi: 10.31579-007/2688-7517/016.

Peck, S.M. (2012) *The Road Less Travelled: A New Psychology of Love, Traditional Values and Spiritual Growth*, 25th edn. New York: Simon & Schuster.

Pedler, M. (2011) *Action Learning in Practice*, 4th edn. London: Gower.

Piercy, F.P., Sprenkle, D.H. and Wetchler, J.L. (1996) *Family Therapy Sourcebook*, 2nd edn. New York: Guilford Press.

Pietrabissa, G., Manzoni, G.M., Rossi, A. and Castelnuovo, G. (2017) The MOTIV-HEART study: a prospective, randomized, single-blind pilot study of brief strategic therapy and motivational interviewing among cardiac rehabilitation patients, *Frontiers in Psychology*, 8: 83.

Pimentel, C.F. and Cravo, M.R. (2013) Goal-based denial and wishful thinking, *IEEE Computational Intelligence Magazine*, 8(2): 63–76.

Pitt, T., Thomas, O., Lindsay, P., Hanton, S. and Bawden, M. (2015) Doing sport psychology briefly? A critical review of single session therapeutic approaches and their relevance to sport psychology, *International Review of Sport and Exercise Psychology*, 8(1): 125–55.

Priest, S. and Gass, M. (1997) An examination of 'problem-solving' versus 'solution-focused' facilitation styles in a corporate setting, *Journal of Experiential Education*, 20(1): 34–39.

Queraltó, J.M. (2006) Metaphors in cognitive behavioural psychology, *Papeles del Psicólogo*, 27(2): 116–22.

Quick, E. (1994) Strategic-solution-focused therapy: a combined approach, *Journal of Systemic Therapies*, 13(1): 74–75.

Quick, E. (2008) *Doing What Works in Brief Therapy: A Strategic Solution Focused Approach*, 2nd edn. San Diego, CA: Academic Press.

Quick, E. (2012) *Core Competencies in the Solution-Focused and Strategic Therapies: Becoming a Highly Competent Solution-Focused and Strategic Therapist*. New York: Taylor & Francis.

Rakowska, J.M. (2015) Brief strategic therapy in first myocardial infarction patients with increased levels of stress: a randomized clinical trial, *Anxiety Stress Coping*, 28(6): 687–705.

Ray, W.A. (2004) Interaction focused therapy: the Don Jackson legacy, *Brief Strategic and Systemic Therapy European Review*, 1: 36–45.

Ray, W.A. (2007) Bateson's cybernetics: the basis of MRI brief therapy: Prologue, *Kybernetes*, 36: 859–70.

Ray, W. (ed.) (2009) *Interactional Theory in the Practice of Therapy: Don D. Jackson, MD, Selected Papers, Volume II*. Phoenix, AZ: Zeig, Tucker & Theisan.

Ray, W.A. and Schangler, K. (2012) John H. Weakland: an interview in retrospect, *Journal of Systemic Therapies*, 31(1): 53–73.

Ray, W.A. (2016) Theory and practice of systemic therapy: a re-introduction to Jackson and Weakland's 'Cojoint family therapy' (1961), *Journal of Systemic Therapies*, 34(4): 29–32.

Ray W.A (2018) The Palo Alto Group, in J. Lebow, A. Chambers and D. Breunlin (eds), *Encyclopedia of Couple and Family Therapy*. Cham: Springer

Rieber, R. and Vetter, H. (1995) The double-bind concept and Gregory Bateson, in *The Psychopathology of Language and Cognition*. Boston, MA: Springer.

Roffman, A.E. (2008) Men are grass: Bateson, Erickson, utilization and metaphor, *American Journal of Clinical Hypnosis*, 50(3): 247–57.

Rohrbaugh, M.J. and Shoham, V. (2001) Brief therapy based on interrupting ironic processes: the Palo Alto model, *Clinical Psychology*, 8(1): 66–81.

Rohrbaugh, M.J. (2014) Old wine in new bottles: decanting systemic family process research in the era of evidence-based practice, *Family Process*, 53(3): 434–44.

Rohrbaugh, M.J. and Shoham, V. (2015) Brief strategic couple therapy, in A.S. Gurman, J.L. Lebow and D.K. Snyder (eds), *Clinical Handbook of Couple Therapy*. New York: Guilford Press.

Rohrbaugh M.J. (2018) Brief strategic couple therapy, in J. Lebow, A. Chambers and D. Breunlin (eds), *Encyclopedia of Couple and Family Therapy*. Cham: Springer.

Rosenbaum, R., Hoyt, M. and Talmon, M. (1990) The challenge of single-session psychotherapies: creating pivotal moments, in R. Wells and V. Gianetti (eds), *Handbook of the Brief Psychotherapies*. New York: Plenum.

Ruby, J. (2018) Paradox in strategic couple and family therapy, in J. Lebow, A. Chambers and D. Breunlin (eds), *Encyclopedia of Couple and Family Therapy*. Cham: Springer.

Russel, W.P. (2017) Directives in couple and family therapy, in J. Lebow, A. Chambers and D. Breunlin (eds), *Encyclopedia of Couple and Family Therapy*. Cham: Springer.

Saggese, M.L. and Foley, F.W. (2000) From problems or solutions to problems and solutions: integrating the MRI and solution-focused models of brief therapy, *Journal of Systemic Therapies*, 19(1): 59–73.

Sandars, J. (2006). Transformative learning: the challenge for reflective practice. *Work based Learning in Primary Care*, 4(1): 6–10.

Schön, D.A. (1987). *Educating the reflective practitioner*. San Francisco, CA: Josey-Bass.

Schöttke, H., Trame, L. and Sembill, A. (2014) Relevance of therapy goals in outpatient cognitive-behavioral and psychodynamic psychotherapy, *Psychotherapy Research*, 24(6): 711–23.

Segal, L. (1991) Brief therapy: the MRI approach, in A.S. Gurman and D.P. Kniskern (eds), *Handbook of Family Therapy, Volume 2*. New York: Brunner-Mazel.

Serrat, O. (2017) *Knowledge Solutions*. Singapore: Springer.

Sheldon, K.M. and Elliot, A.J. (1999) Goal striving, need satisfaction, and longitudinal wellbeing, *Journal of Personality and Social Psychology*, 76(3): 482–97.

Shoham, V., Rohrbaugh, M. and Patterson, J. (1995) Problem- and solution-focused couple therapies: the MRI and Milwaukee models, in N.S. Jacobson and A.S. Gurman (eds), *Clinical Handbook of Couple Therapy*. New York: Guilford Press.

Short, D., Erickson, B.A. and Erickson-Klein, R. (2005) *Hope and Resiliency: Understanding the Therapeutic Strategies of Milton H. Erickson*. Carmathen: Crown House Publishing.

Sigall, H., Kruglanski, A. and Fyock, J. (2000) Wishful thinking and procrastination, *Journal of Social Behavior and Personality*, 15: 283–96.

Soo-Hoo, T. (1997) Strategic consultation: the evolution and application of an efficient approach, *Consulting Psychology Journal: Practice and Research*, 49(3): 194–206.

Stelter, R. and Law, H. (2010) Coaching – narrative-collaborative practice, *Coaching Psychology Review*, 5(2): 152–64.

Stelter, R. (2013) Narrative approaches, in J. Passmore, D.B. Peterson and T. Freire (eds), *The Wiley-Blackwell Handbook of the Psychology of Coaching and Mentoring*. Chichester: John Wiley.

Sullivan, H.S. (1953). *The interpersonal theory of psychiatry*. New York: Norton.

Taylor, D. (2020). Reflective practice in the art and science of counselling: a scoping review. *Psychotherapy and Counselling Journal of Australia*, 8: 1–14.

Tomm, K. (1988) Interventive interviewing: Part III. Intending to ask lineal, circular, reflexive or strategic questions?, *Family Process*, 27: 1–15.

Torbert, W. and Associates (2004) *Action Inquiry: The Secret of Timely and Transforming Leadership*. San Francisco, CA: Berrett-Koehler Publishers.

Tramonti, F. (2018) Steps to an ecology of psychotherapy: the legacy of Gregory Bateson, *Systems Research and Behavioral Science*, 36(1): 128–39.

Vaughn, M. (2004) Creating 'maneuvering room': a grounded theory of language and influence in marriage and family therapy, *Contemporary Family Therapy*, 26(4): 426–45.

Visser, C.F. (2013) The origin of the solution-focused approach, *International Journal of Solution-Focused Practices*, 1(1): 10–17.

Vitry, G., Duriez, N., Lartilleux-Suberville, S., Pakrosnis, R., Beau, A., Garcia-Rivera, T., Brosseau, O., Vargas Avalos, P., Bardot, E. and Ray, W.A. (2020) Introducing

SYPRENE: an international practice research network for strategic and systemic therapists and researchers, *Family Process*, 59(4): 1946–57.

Volz-Peacock, M., Carson, B. and Marquardt, M. (2016) Action learning and leadership development, *Advances in Developing Human Resources*, 18(3): 318–33.

Wachtel, E.F. and Wachtel, P.L. (1986) *Family Dynamics in Individual Psychotherapy*. New York: Guilford Press.

Watzlawick, P. (1963) A review of the double bind theory, *Family Process*, 2(1): 132–53.

Watzlawick, P. (1976) *How Real is Real? Confusion, Disinformation, Communication*. New York: Vintage Books.

Watzlawick, P. and Weakland, J.H. (eds) (1977) *The Interactional View*. New York: W.W. Norton.

Watzlawick, P. (1978) *The Language of Change: Elements of Therapeutic Conversations*. New York: Basic Books.

Watzlawick, P. and Coyne, J.C. (1980) Depression following stroke: brief, problem-focused family treatment, *Family Process*, 19(1): 13–18.

Watzlawick. P. (1988) *Ultrasolutions: How to Fail Most Successfully*. New York: W.W. Norton.

Watzlawick, P., Bavelas, J.B. and Jackson, D.D. (2011; original work published 1967) *Pragmatics of Human Communication: A Study of Interactional Patterns, Pathologies and Paradoxes*. New York: W.W. Norton.

Watzlawick, P., Weakland, J.H. and Fisch, R. (2011; original work published 1974) *Change: Principles of Problem Formation and Problem Solution*. New York: W.W. Norton.

Weakland, J.H., Fisch, R., Watzlawick, P. and Bodin, A. (1974) Brief therapy: focused problem resolution, *Family Process*, 13(2): 141–68.

Weakland, J.H. (1979) The double-bind theory: some current implications for child psychiatry, *Journal of the American Academy of Child Psychiatry*, 18(1): 54–66.

Weakland, J.H. and Ray, W.A. (eds) (1995) *Propagations: Thirty Years of Influence from the Mental Research Institute*. New York: Haworth Press.

Weakland, J.H and Fisch, R. (2010) The strategic approach, *Journal of Systemic Therapies*, 29(4): 29–34.

Weeks, G.R. (ed.) (2013) *Promoting Change through Paradoxical Therapy*. Chevy Chase, MD: International Psychotherapy Institute.

Weeks, G.R. and L'Abate, L. (1982) *Paradoxical Psychotherapy. Theory and Practice with Individuals Couples and Families*. New York: Routledge.

West, J.D., Main, F.O. and Zarski, J.J. (1986) The paradoxical prescription in individual psychology, *Individual Psychology*, 42(2): 214–24.

White, M. and Epston, D. (1990) *Narrative Means to Therapeutic Ends*. New York: W.W. Norton.

Whybrow, A. and Palmer, S. (2006) Taking stock: a survey of coaching psychologists' practices and perspectives, *International Coaching Psychology Review*, 1(1): 56–70.

Yapko, M.D. (2015) *Essentials of Hypnosis*, 2nd edn. New York: Routledge.

Yapko, M.D. (2019) *Trancework: An Introduction to the Practice of Clinical Hypnosis*, 5th edn. New York: Routledge.

Zeig, J.K. (2006a) *Confluence: The Selected Papers of Jeffrey K. Zeig – Volume 1*. Phoenix, AZ: Zeig, Tucker & Theisen.

Zeig, J.K. (2006b) Using tasks in Ericksonian psychotherapy, in W. O'Donohue, N.A. Cummings and J.L. Cummings (eds.), *Critical Strategies for Becoming a Master Psychotherapist: A Volume in Practical Resources for the Mental Health Professional*. Burlington, MA: Academic Press.

Zeig, J.K. (2014) *The Induction of Hypnosis: An Ericksonian Elicitation Approach*. Phoenix, AZ: The Milton H. Erickson Foundation Press.

Index

Page numbers in italics are figures; with 't' are tables.